Also By Lee Silber

The Wild Idea Club

Rock to Riches: Build Your Business the Rock & Roll Way

Chicken Soup for the Beach Lover's Soul (Contributor)

Confessions of Shameless Self-Promoters (Contributor)

Organizing from the Right Side of the Brain

Money-Management for the Creative Person

Self-Promotion for the Creative Person

Career-Management for the Creative Person

Time-Management for the Creative Person

Summer Stories

LEE SILBER + MIKE METZ

BORED GAMES

SIMPLE FUN FROM YOUR POCKET OR PURSE—ANYWHERE, ANYTIME

Capital Ideas Series

CAPITAL
BOOKS, INC.
Sterling, Virginia

Capital Books, Inc.
P.O. Box 605
Herndon, Virginia 20172-0605

ISBN 13: 978-1-933102-83-2

Library of Congress Cataloging-in-Publication Data

Silber, Lee T.
  Bored games : simple fun from your pocket or purse anytime, anywhere / Lee Silber and Mike Metz. -- 1st ed.
     p. cm.
  ISBN 978-1-933102-83-2 (alk. paper)
 1. Games. 2. Amusements. I. Metz, Mike. II. Title.

  GV1201.S488 2009
  793--dc22

                          2009014997

Printed in the United States of America on acid-free paper that meets the American National Standards Institute Z39-48 Standard.

First Edition

10 9 8 7 6 5 4 3 2 1

Cover and interior design: Lee Silber

This book is dedicated to anyone who wants to have a deeper connection and more fun with their friends and family.

ACKNOWLEDGMENTS

THANK YOU

To my late father, a more resourceful person you could not meet. He could take almost anything (broken or not) and find ten other uses for it. To my mom, who taught me all about arts and crafts, and papier-mâché volcanoes. To my brothers, who played roll-dice baseball (and other invented games) with me until the wee hours of the morning while growing up—and last week. To my wife, who carried a giant purse for over a year to schlep the stuff used in the making of this book—and endured everything from spitball wars to bug-collecting contests. To my boys, Ethan and Evan, who took nearly every one of the activities in this book for a test drive—and offered their brutally honest opinions (solicited or not). To my friend Mark Bromley, who (ten years ago) left his kids with me at the beach while he ran errands because (and I quote), "You are like the best Daddy Daycare in the world." That's when I started keeping a notebook with ideas for this book. Finally, to everyone at Capital Books (Kathleen, Amy, Jean, and Jane) who believed in this book and its power to cure boredom. Thank you all. —**LEE**

To my best friend, my wife Paige, who has put up with many of my shenanigans, whether we experienced them together through our family, or by helping clean up the mess afterwards—"life will never be dull." To my daughter (Kragen) and son (M.J.), who were instrumental in inspiring the defeat of boredom at the beach, park, or trying to nap on the couch—"and don't forget . . ." To my parents, for always being there as a sounding board, providing guidance, being great examples, and teaching me the infinitesimal uses of a rock and a stick—"stop bouncing that ball in here." Finally to my good friend Lee, who is the most optimistic person I know—"stop finishing my sentences for me." —**MIKE**

CONTENTS

It's really fast and easy to find the perfect game or activity to best suit the situation at hand—the kids are bored and you need to find something to do . . . fast—since we listed everything alphabetically and numerically.

There are 70 different games and activities listed here to help you and those around you beat boredom—and it gets better. On each page we provide variations and options so you can play the same game a different way, or take an activity and customize it for the setting or situation you find yourself in. So really, there are hundreds of ways to pass the time and create magic moments with family and friends.

NUMBER / ACTIVITY

1 Admiration
2 Amazed
3 Backhanded Compliment
4 Battleground
5 Belong, or Not Belong?
6 Birthday Wishes

NUMBER / ACTIVITY

7 Bingo-A-Go-Go
8 Blindfolded
9 Bored Games
10 Bombs Away
11 Bowling For Dollars
12 Bring A Book To Life

NUMBER / ACTIVITY	NUMBER / ACTIVITY
13 Bubble Gum Blowing	25 Fun With Food
14 Bug Me	26 Guessing Games
15 Bull's Eye	27 Hangin' Around
16 Card Sharks	28 Heads Up
17 Con-Cencus Poll	29 Hoop Dreams
18 Creativity Added	30 Huh?
19 Custom Cups	31 It's In The Bag
20 Dicey	32 Jack And Jill
21 Doctor Doctor	33 King Of The Circle
22 Family Tree	34 Knot Exactly
23 Favorite Things	35 Last Laugh
24 Finger Fun	36 Last Straw

NUMBER / ACTIVITY	NUMBER / ACTIVITY
37 Liar's Club	49 Pencil Pusher
38 Long Jump	50 Perspective
39 Mind Reader	51 Pile It Up
40 Movie Magic	52 Pump It Up
41 Musical Menus	53 Rave Reviews
42 Name That Tune	54 Scrappy
43 Napkin Dreams	55 Scavengers
44 Nature Lover	56 Science
45 Newlywed Game	57 Shooting Gallery
46 Oprah	58 Shopping Spree
47 Parent Trap	59 Sock Me
48 Pass It On	60 Table Tennis

LET'S HAVE FUN

Do these sayings sound familiar: "Are we there yet?" and "What's taking so long?" How many times have you been somewhere and the kids (or adults behaving like kids) are "acting up" because they are fidgety, fighting with each other, or worse, their fingers are so busy sending text messages they completely ignore you? Ever looked at your watch (and even tapped it) wondering if it was working because time was going by soooooo slow? *Bored Games* is filled with ideas to turn these challenging times into magic moments where everyone is laughing, learning, and having the time of their lives. You will also be inspired to create your own unique boredom-busters—activities and memories that will last a lifetime.

ANYWHERE, ANYTIME

Because the ideas and activities in *Bored Games* are based on items already in your pocket and purse, you can do them anywhere, anytime. *And best of all—they're free.*

FOR KIDS OF ALL AGES AND STYLES

Bored Games is packed full of battle-tested ways to engage and entertain kids of any age and personality. Whether a child is outgoing or shy, easily distracted or intently focused, or is analytical or naturally creative—we include games for everyone.

TURN COMMUTING TIME INTO QUALITY TIME

Between having to work more hours than ever to make ends meet and schlepping the kids here and there in your "free time"—everyone is harried and hurried. Now, you can enjoy the journey and turn what was once considered wasted time into the time of your life. The ideas in this book can turn even the most mundane activities into adventures. In the process, you can teach children dozens of valuable lessons—like how to be resourceful and creative—for less than the cost of a movie ticket or store-bought toy. It's a way to get things done *and* still have some fun.

DON'T WAIT IN LINE—PLAY IN LINE

In many areas of the country, there seems to be too many people who all want to do the same thing at the same time. This means we're all waiting in line—at restaurants, doctors' offices, and stores. *Bored Games* turns these otherwise dull and dreary times into a treat. Kids who were once bored and hard to handle are now entertained and excited to the point of wanting to wait even longer. Time truly does fly by when you're having fun.

GOOD OLD HEALTHY FUN (BUT DON'T TELL THE KIDS!)

Kids who need their own day planners to keep up with their busy schedules are missing out on something that is equally important as any planned activity, and that is free play and creative freedom. This book inspires both by encouraging kids to use their imagination and what's around them to have fun—which also means less time spent on television and video games. (Parents and grandparents will really appreciate this old school approach.) In addition, many of the fun and creative things to do in *Bored Games* include physical activity. But don't tell the kids the games are healthy. It's sort of like hiding healthy food inside foods kids like. They won't even realize this book is "good for them"—they'll just be having fun.

GOOD FOR PARENTS AND OTHER CAREGIVERS

Though *Bored Games* is mostly for the kids' amusement, parents will love it too. This book is a major stress reducer. When you put these ideas to use, you'll see that stress, anger, crankiness and boredom are replaced by joy, laughter, creativity, and fun—and that's just what the adults are feeling. It's even better for kids. This book won't just keep your kids busy for a few hours, but days if you want to. As a bonus—implementing the ideas and activities in this book instantly makes you the fun friend, cool parent, hip grandparent, amazing nanny, awesome teacher, the inspirational daycare provider, and the favorite aunt or uncle.

FAMILIES THAT PLAY TOGETHER . . .

While many activities in this book can be done independently by young readers, they're equally as entertaining when done as a group. They'll remind you just how much fun play can be—at any age. How can we be so sure? We've witnessed it with our own eyes and ears. We've used all of these boredom busters and they work. It's thrilling to see kids having a ball while using and expanding their imagination, knowledge and creativity. It's also gratifying to watch adults getting in touch with their inner child and connecting with kids on a deeper level.

WHAT ARE YOU WAITING FOR?

You hold in your hand a book packed full of tried and tested ways to engage and entertain kids using things you already have—at no additional cost to you. This book does much more than entertain kids. It also:

Brings families together

Inspires and rewards creativity

Builds self-esteem

Teaches lifelong lessons

Creates positive memories

Keeps kids active physically and mentally

Encourages children to think analytically

Fosters independent thinking

Not many books do all that—this one does. So, what are you waiting for, go have fun!

CHECKLIST

While this list makes it look like you'll need a larger pocket or purse, many of the things you'll need for these activities are already right at your fingertips, just look around. But just in case, you can carry some of the "rarer" items on this list with you.

Balls	Balloons	Blindfold	Books	Camera	Candy
Cell Phone	Clothespins	Coins	Cotton Balls	Crayons	Deck of Cards
Dice	Glue	Gum	Hanky	Ink Pad	Keys
Paper	Paper Clips	Pens/Pencils	Plastic Bags	Rubber Bands	Scissors
Socks	Straws	String	Timer	Watch	Water

LET'S GO

THE GAMES

Here you will find over 100 different ways to beat boredom and win affection from kids and adults. What's great about *Bored Games* is how quickly you can make time go from frustrating to fun. One of the reasons it's so simple is the way this book is designed. All you have to do is skim the pages looking for something that jumps out at you, then let the fun begin. In fact, you can open to any page and just go with whatever you land on, because you can trust that every idea in this book has been put to the test—and passed. Keep in mind, some ideas may seem silly (to an adult) but give them a try anyway, because these were really written for the kids—and the kid in all of us.

Admiration

A discussion and game using your heroes.

1

You can learn a lot about someone when you know who they admire—and they will discover something about themselves, too. In this activity you can keep it simple and just ask each person to name someone they admire and why. Or, each person can give some clues about their hero and see if others can guess who it is.

This activity can be played anywhere—in the car, on a plane, during dinner, or in a waiting room. If there are others around you want to meet, these questions make a great icebreaker. At home, these can be done as a book report, where each family member does a presentation about their favorite person complete with facts and figures.

HOW TO PLAY

Start a discussion about the most impressive people you can think of. (These can be real people—alive or dead—or fictional character and superheroes.) Then go around the room and ask each person to name the one person they admire most. Have the person tell you everything they know about their hero. You can make the game more informative and interesting by adding the following questions.

1. What is it about your hero that inspires you?
2. What do they have (or do) that you don't? Why is this important to you?
3. What do you have in common with them? What have they done that you want to?
4. Would you want to trade places for a day? What would you do? If not, why?
5. If you could meet them, what would you say? What would you do for a day?
6. If your hero was here with us right now, what would he/she do?
7. Can you think of something about this person that others should know, but don't?

WHAT YOU NEED

For the advanced version: Internet access to look up the person on Wikipedia, or Google to create trivia/true and false questions.

BONUS

You can adjust this game for each age group. Really young kids can use superheroes, older kids can pick someone they learned about in school or have seen on television, and for adults you can give some parameters to pick from.

Amazed

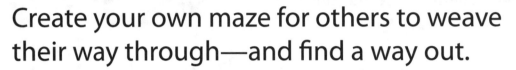

Create your own maze for others to weave their way through—and find a way out.

Creating a maze for others to solve is fun for both the person creating it and the person navigating it. The object is to confuse the player by making twists and turns that lead nowhere, but also make sure they have at least one way out. The age group that likes this type of activity is five to infinity. Almost everyone likes to solve the problem posed by a maze.

HOW TO PLAY

Mazes are made simply with pen and paper. Whether you use a circle or square to start, the key is to have a plan as to where the person begins and ends the maze. Other than that, go crazy.

WHAT YOU NEED

Just a paper and pen. We say "pen" because a "creative" player could erase a pencil line here or there to create their own easy exit.

BONUS

Of course this is easier to do on paper, but you can create a maze using actual objects— furniture, pillows, potted plants, taped lines on the floor, etc. This makes the activity more physical since the participants are working their way through your maze/obstacle course with their feet.

Backhanded Compliment

Carry as much small stuff on the back of your hand as you can—while racing the clock.

You're probably thinking, how hard can it be to carry some small stuff on the back of my hand? We can tell you, it's harder than it seems—especially if you turn this into a game of speed and agility. There are several ways to play this game, but the basic premise is the same—see how much stuff you can carry across a room on the back of your hand (without dropping anything). As you will read below, this can be fun for two people . . . or more.

HOW TO PLAY

1. The most basic way to play is to put a pile of small items from your pocket or purse on the table. Then each person, in turn, piles as much as they think they can carry on the back of their hand to see how far they can walk without dropping anything. Mark the spot, and the next player must make it past that spot to win.

2. Pit two people against one another in a race—who can get from one spot to another the fastest without anything falling from the back of their hand.

3. This could be a team event with four or more people. The object of this version of the game is for each team member to make it from one side of the room and dump the contents from the back of their hand into a bowl, then race back so the next player on their team gets a turn. The first team that fills their bowl wins.

WHAT YOU NEED

Small odds and ends from your pocket or purse and a steady hand.

Battleground

A healthy dose of good old-fashioned fun, and a couple of "war" games.

For years boys have held mock battles, whether it be sword fights, Army skirmishes, or Cowboys versus Indians. We're not saying this is perfectly okay, we're just saying it happens. And it's not just the boys who do this. The girls have been known to mix it up too. So here are a couple of ways to "play" around with this concept.

HOW TO PLAY

1. **Civil War Style.** Line up and create two areas with a line down the middle separating the two "countries"—one team in each country. Try to get to the other side of the

room (or over a line) without being touched by the other team. The "Army" that gets the most soldiers across untouched wins. You have to stay within the boundaries (narrow). The strategy can be to try and touch the other team players to eliminate them or make a mad dash for the other side. Or, each team simply tries to cross enemy territory to capture the other's flag (a T-shirt tied to a tree.)

2. **Navy SEALS.** The object of this game is to be as stealthy as possible so you can sneak up on others in the group. For example, at the beach a couple of "SEALS" can sneak off (with an adult leading the attack) and try to circle around and surprise the rest of the group. Or, a couple of "SEALS" hide while the others try to seek and destroy them (point out where they are hiding).

3. **Pirate Ship/Smuggler's Blues.** This game requires either tape or rope to outline two or more pirate ships on the ground. Teams are made up and assigned a ship, which is filled with coins, wood chips, or pebbles. The object is to get all of your "treasure" off the ship before the other team does so you can "sail away safely." What makes it more

interesting is if each team throws their contraband onto the other ship to prevent them from unloading first—thus sinking them.

4. **Sword Fights.** Using something soft as swords (such as rolled-up newspapers), set up a circle where two players try to force the other person outside the lines using nothing more than their sword. If the sword touches part of their body, they can't use it.

6. **Cowboys and Indians.** This can actually be politically correct when the "cowboys and cowgirls" work together with the Indians. In this game (clearly aimed at a younger player) most of the kids are wild horses and the object is for the cowboys and Indians to partner up to round up the "horses" and corral them.

5. **Bombs Away.** There is nothing as epic as snowball battles in the winter and water balloon fights in the summer.

WHAT YOU NEED

Tape, rope, coins, water balloons.

Belong Or Not Belong

Add one or more things to a room or a table and see who can guess what doesn't belong.

First you add an item[s] to a room or a table, trying to trick others who have to figure out and find the things that weren't there before. You can do this in a restaurant, a waiting room, outside, in the car, your office, almost anywhere. There are other variations of this simple but fun game below, so take a look at "Back-to-Back" and "Like Me" for more ideas.

HOW TO PLAY

1. **One Too Many.** If this game is played in a place everyone has been to before, the best bet is to add things that don't belong before they arrive. If it's somewhere you are all seeing for the first time, tell everyone to either leave the room or close their eyes while you run around and add additional items to the room or table. Obviously, the best bet is stashing stuff that goes up quickly—stickers, a flower brought in from outside, a pen put out in plain sight (that wasn't there before).

2. **Back-to-Back.** Another variation on this game is to have everyone turn back-to-back so they can't see one another. Then each person must change three things about their appearance—remove their glasses, switch a ring from finger to finger, pick something up and hold it. Then when the players face each other again, they must correctly guess what's different.

3. **Like Me.** Put together a group of items that all go together (car keys, driver's license, and a proof-of-insurance card) but add in one that does not belong (a saltshaker, wa-

ter bottle, beer bottle?) and see who can figure out the odd item. You can do the same with food items and teach kids about the different food groups. (We all know pizza can cover at least four food groups, right?)

WHAT YOU NEED

An item or items to be added to the room. Almost any item—from the fridge or the table, for example—will work.

Bingo On The Go-Go

This game is a little like regular bingo, except it's played in the car, with landmarks.

Each player has their own "Bingo" sheet with several boxes, each of which includes a drawing (or the word) of a different item they must spot while in the car—and check off. The first person to find everything on their list, wins. This game proves that time flies when you're having fun and can be played on a long road trip or just a jaunt around town running errands. It's also a teaching tool and improves people's powers of observation.

HOW TO PLAY

1. The first step is to take a guess at what you think you will see while driving. Depending on the landscape, this could be anything from a traffic light or a truck to a Starbucks or McDonald's. You then either write in or draw these on a sheet of paper marked with bingo boxes. (Each player should have a different set of items to look for.)

2. The things that are featured can make the game incredibly easy or very hard. If you include a rare sea bird and a fishing boat in a city that is miles from the water, well . . . The same goes for a rural area where it's unlikely to see a jet or a ten-story building.

3. Travel bingo can also be played anywhere people gather. This version is more about people instead of places and things. The goal can be to look for someone old, young, blonde, brunette, black, white, and so on. The lesson here is how diverse we are.

WHAT YOU NEED

Paper and pens (or crayons).

Birthday Wishes

7

This activity is about creating the ultimate birthday wish list using a variety of methods.

If there is one topic that can get people talking, it's what they want for Christmas or their birthday. This activity helps people focus not only on what they want (and don't have) but also what they can be thankful for (what they already have). Depending on how elaborate you want to make this undertaking, it can be done just about anywhere, anytime. It's especially good to play just before a person's birthday or the holidays. You now won't have to wonder what your friends and family want for the holidays or their next birthday.

HOW TO PLAY

There are a number of ways to start this discussion, but the easiest is to just go around the table and ask each person what they would want for their birthday if price were no object. You can then follow that up with:

1. If price were an object what would you want? What is the best thing you could get for under ten bucks? What is the best gift you have ever gotten? The worst gift?

2. You can also have people use magazines and catalogs to tear or cut out the things they would want and tape or glue them to a piece of paper. It's a lot like a ransom note, but you don't have to comply—kind of like a birthday collage.

3. You can have people make a list of all the things they would want to get as a gift, but not put their name on it. These lists would then be put into a pile and randomly chosen. The next phase is to guess which wish list goes with whom.

4. Instead of asking people what they want, ask them what their most prized posses-

sion is? What they are most grateful for? What is priceless in their life?

WHAT YOU NEED

If you keep it simple, nothing. Or, you can use crayons, markers, magazines, catalogs, paper, scissors, and glue.

Blindfolded

8

Here are a number of things that can be made more fun while blindfolded.

When you picture someone being blindfolded, it can either be beautiful (a surprise) or horrific (we won't go there). Let's focus on the positive with some really cool ways to make something seem fresh and new by using a blindfold. Make up your own game or adventure where adding the element of surprise (or lack of sight) would make it more interesting.

HOW TO PLAY

1. **Marco Polo.** For kids—they will get a kick out of playing "Marco Polo" on land. The

"it" person is blindfolded and must find (and tag) the others who are not blindfolded and must answer "Polo" when the person who is "it" and blindfolded says, "Marco."

2. **Blinded by the Dark.** Another fun game is to have teams with one participant blindfolded while the other team members give verbal instructions to guide them to find an object, race to a finish line, or both.

3. **Clueless.** Blindfold a person before leaving the house. Then lead that person outside and have him or her guess where they are being led by the clues they hear (a train goes by, the crowd roars at a ballgame, the sound of the surf).

4. **Lights Out.** How about dinner in the dark? Everyone is blindfolded and tries to eat without being able to see. Or one person is blindfolded and the others guide them.

5. **See the Light.** For someone who thinks their life is tough (a teenager) and they have nothing to be happy about—blindfold them (with their permission, of course) for a short time so they can "see the light" and appreciate what they take for granted.

6. **Operating in the Dark.** This is definitely one of those "touchy feely" games. One

way to play is to blindfold a participant; then they must figure out who is who in the room by "feeling out" each person's features. Or, two blindfolded people stand apart from one another and try to guess each other's body parts by feel alone. The person who can name the most body parts in a minute, wins.

7. **Pin the Money on the Wall.** Here are two classic birthday party games that can be revised for everyday use. One is Pin the Tail on the Donkey, and the other is the piñata. You can substitute a pin with sticky notes to stick on a wall. And then associate spots on the wall with various things a person has to do if they post a sticky note there. These tasks could range from hug your mother to kiss your brother. For the piñata, fill a paper bag with goodies and see who can hit it hard enough to break it loose.

WHAT YOU NEED

A handkerchief works best, but a large napkin or dark shirt can do the trick to "blind-fold" someone.

Board Games

Invent your own version of a classic board game.

Making up your own board game based on one you already know (*Monopoly*, *PayDay*, *Sorry!*) is pretty simple and straightforward. The great thing is that you need nothing more than a pair of dice, paper, and some pawns to move around. Combine rules from many existing games, copy one specific game, or create your own brand new game. Creating your own game is both fun and easy—and the best part is you make the rules!

HOW TO PLAY

1. The best games are chase games—where you create a series of squares on paper to

advance based on the roll of the dice. What makes it more interesting are the pitfalls (or rewards) you put in along the way (go to jail, move ahead 10 spaces, go to timeout for 60 seconds, chug a cup of juice). Kids really get a chance to use their imagination on filling in the squares, or they can all be filled in by one person—like on a rainy/snowy day while dad is watching the football game.

2. Another option for creating your own game is to make a path of squares and leave them all blank when you start. Then as players roll and move along the path, whichever spot they land on they get to fill in the square with whatever rule they want. You can have a theme that everyone follows (eating, drinking, silly truth-or-dare tasks) or physical challenges (run up the stairs and back, do a summersault, switch articles of clothing)—the theme can depend on the season, time of day, or location.

3. Another fun board game to base your game on is *The Game of Life*. Now you can entertain and educate at the same time. This game teaches kids the importance of getting an education (jump ahead two spaces), staying out of debt (get another turn),

waiting to get married, and so on, all reflected on the game "board" you create.

4. The game *Battleship* is always a hit. You can create grids with boxes (graphs) on paper with letters along the left and numbers running across the bottom. Then have players draw in their battleships up and down or across the boxes of their choice. Like the real game, you call out a number and letter combination (B-2) and see if you can hit (and sink) their battleship. Add as many boats as you need for the amount of time you are waiting.

WHAT YOU NEED

Depending on the type of board game you decide to create, you may need dice, paper, pens, something to use as place holders (coins, keys, and candy work well), and maybe good running shoes.

Bombs Away

This game is a lot like "hot potato" and "hide and seek," but with a modern twist.

There are two ways to play this game. The first is using anything with a timer or alarm on it—cell phone, watch, or an egg timer (if you happen to have one). Then the item that could go off at any minute is passed around and the person holding it when it buzzes is eliminated. The second way to play the game is to hide the (phone, watch, timer) somewhere and kids work as a team to find it before it goes off.

HOW TO PLAY

1. Hide the egg timer and kids can follow the ticking sound to find it wherever you

have hidden it—thye have to find it before it detonates (rings).

2. If you use a watch or cell phone with an alarm, they must locate it before it buzzes, but they won't have a clue like the ticking egg timer to follow.

3. Try giving the team a chance to deactivate the device before it goes off. This will teach them about the functions on a phone or a watch––or they'll teach you.

4. Using any device that has an alarm, you set it to go off in 30 seconds or a minute and start passing it around. The object is to not be the one holding it when it goes off.

5. Use the cell phone of someone who gets a LOT of calls (or text messages) and each person has to hold it for half a minute and hope it doesn't ring while in their hand.

6. Many restaurants now give you a pager that buzzes and lights up when your table is ready. Pass it around, and the person holding it when it goes off wins (or loses).

WHAT YOU NEED

The best "bombs" have a loud alarm so those searching will know when it's activated.

Bowling For Dollars

This isn't a bowling alley, but more like bowling in an alley.

Bowling is one sport that is easy to emulate. If you line up ten bottles, cans, or plastic cups in a triangular arrangement and roll a round object at them, you're bowling. That's what we are suggesting here. There really is no age limit on this game as long as your nonbreakable empties are truly empty. Also, this is best done outside and preferably not on a steep hill.

HOW TO PLAY

1. Empty, nonbreakable cans and bottles work best as surrogate bowling pins. The best pseudo bowling balls are baseballs. That said, almost anything tall and thin that stands on end will do as a pin (as long as you have ten of them), and any round object (an orange works well) can be the ball. We find it's a lot easier to keep it simple (only your first roll counts, no picking up spares), and you simply score each pin as one point.
2. You can create a miniature table version of this game using a small ball and items from a purse (lipstick, mascara, pill container—anything that is tall and will stand on end.) You can give extra points for hard-to-knock down pins (full water bottles) and take away points for knocking down the dreaded evil pin (dad's full soda).

WHAT YOU NEED

What you need is covered in "How To Play," but we will add this caveat, glass bottles break, and once an apple has been rolled around a few times, it won't taste very good.

Bring A Book To Life

12

By re-creating and acting out the parts in a book, the "actors" can bring the words to life.

Many books are made into movies. This is your chance to bring a book to life by acting out what you see (think picture books for small kids) or acting like the characters contained on the pages. The best part is, you can do this almost anywhere. (If you are one of those people who gets motion sickness from reading in a car, this activity may come back up on you.) The game can also be adjusted for different age groups and done a number of different ways. Unless a person is in a drama class, this is a rare chance to act in a play. Also, reading aloud is a learned skill and practice makes perfect.

HOW TO PLAY

1. If you have a book handy, this will be easy. You can either assign a narrator, and everyone else acts out what they hear (good for very little kids who don't read). The narrator can be an over-the-top reader and really bring the book to life with accents, animal sounds, and anything that makes it more interesting. If you have kids who can read, assign them a specific character they can "play."

2. If you don't have a book to use, a newspaper will work. People can act like promoters (bringing the ads to life) or newscasters (reading and reacting to the news), or even form a commentary-type show to discuss the stories of the day.

WHAT YOU NEED

All you really need is a book or a magazine, and you are good to go.

Bubble Gum Blowing Contest

13

A simple contest to see who can blow the biggest bubble.

Most kids will be thrilled when you tell them to stuff as much bubble gum into their mouth as they can and blow the biggest bubble possible.

HOW TO PLAY

1. There are several variations on the premise that the biggest bubble wins. For example, the first one to blow a bubble of any kind wins. There can also be a winner

for the most unusual looking bubble. Or, the most bubbles blown in a minute gets a prize—more gum? Obviously this isn't a good one in the library or in church, but almost anywhere else is fine. The only rule is don't get the gum in your hair or on the floor. Anyone old enough to meet the guidelines can play.

2. If you happen to have bubble-making materials (you know, the stuff that comes in a container with a little wand that's buried in the slimy goop), you can have contests for biggest bubble, most bubbles, bubble that lasted the longest, most bubbles "caught", bubble that travels the farthest.

WHAT YOU NEED

Bubble gum or bubbles in a jar.

Bug Me

This is more than a bug-collecting contest—it's a science experiment too.

Using plastic cups (or anything that can contain a bug), the kids are sent out to search for the biggest bug, the ugliest bug, or even the rarest bug . . . then the real fun begins. The only rules are: NO stinging, biting bugs; bug containers should have holes for air; and the bugs should be set free at the end of the game.

HOW TO PLAY

1. Once the kids are sent out into the "wild" to look for and capture as many bugs as they can in a predetermined amount of time, they must report back to "class." The

young ophthalmologists will be judged based on their bugs. Prizes will be awarded for the person with the most bugs, the best bugs (rarest, most colorful, biggest), and then their knowledge of their catch. The person that can name all the types of bugs they have dug up will also win. Hopefully, if you are at a restaurant, the bug collection competition will take place outside and stay outside the eatery.

2. If you are a bug lover, look away now. Still here. How about bug races? Pit one worm or snail against another in a crawling contest? (Note, this could take a while.)

3. The funny thing is, many kids will revel in the chance to create their own bug circus. Adults may be squeamish when it comes to creepy crawly stuff, but anyone under the age of thirteen will love it.

WHAT YOU NEED

The main tool is a cup (preferably with a lid) to capture the critters and some sort of hand-washing solution for afterward.

Bull's Eye

This is a safe and simple game of darts using pens and paper.

The object of the game is to drop a pen or pencil from arms length onto a bull's-eye chart made on paper and placed on a flat surface like a floor or a table. Just like regular darts, you score points for accuracy. There are several variations of this game, but they all begin with a pen drop. Here are some of the ways to create your target.

HOW TO PLAY

1. The most straightforward way to play is to make rings with points given for each area—the bull's eye being the best, of course, just like a dart board. The first person to

get to, say, 20 points wins. If they are available, we find using different colored pens for each person is best, but also a luxury. Circle each drop mark and initial them, and then keep score on a separate sheet of paper.

2. The game could also be simplified even further. The winner could be the first one to hit the bull's eye or the first one to come closest to it.

3. To make the game harder, you can draw objects on the page, and each player has to hit each object at least once to win.

WHAT YOU NEED

A pen and paper. Spread newspapers under and around the target if you're playing on a scratchable floor or table.

Card Sharks

These are kid-friendly card games that don't involve (a lot of) gambling.

These are the basic cards games we have all played, but you can add a modern twist to make them a combination of entertainment and learning.

HOW TO PLAY

1. **High Card.** The main game is played shuffling an ordinary deck and then placing one card face-up on the table. Then the player must guess if the next card will be higher or lower. The first player to get it right 51 (or seven) times in a row wins.

2. **Go Fish.** Play the classic game of *Go Fish* but add a twist by picking up two cards at

a time. Or a certain card is an automatic pair. Or play with wild cards.

3. **Crazy Eights.** Everyone gets eight cards, and one is placed face-up next to a pick-'em pile. Players go around the circle following either the suit or number of the face-up card. If you can't play, then pick a card. Eights are wild of course. First one to get rid of their cards wins. Add more cards as wilds to make the game go at an even faster pace.

4. **Slap Jack.** Kids of all ages can play this. As this is a game that never seems to end, you can call a winner when they have all four Jacks. Or change it up and play Slap Kings, Slap Queens, Slap odd numbers, even numbers, etc.

5. **Slap Math.** Make it a quick math game to only slap numbers that add up to ten or eight. Or everyone puts down a card at once and the first person to add up all the numbers, keeps the played cards. The idea is to get the kids quick-thinking on math problems. And you always have a set of flash cards with you.

6. **Add It Up.** Much like a Black Jack game to 21. See how many cards each player can take until they get as close to the 21 total. Or 31. Or 11. Depends on how old the kids

are and how their counting skills are. Use sugar packs as pretend money—all restaurants will love this one (wink).

WHAT YOU NEED

A deck of playing cards. And check out this website for other card game ideas: usplayingcard.com/gamerules/childrenscardgames.html.

Con-Census Poll

By polling passersby or people in line, you can learn a lot—and pass the time.

This is all about fishing out the facts by conducting your own unscientific poll. While waiting in line, it would be fun to ask random people the same question to see what they say—and where the commonalities are.

HOW TO PLAY

1. Using a pad of paper, write your question and leave room for a lot of answers. The questions can be outrageous (what is the worst thing your parents ever grounded you for—and for how long?) or ingenious (if you could go back in time and tell yourself one

thing when you were my age—knowing what you know now—what would it be?) Log all answers, tally the results, and share the findings with all. Topics that elicit good responses are: birthday months, zodiac signs, birth order, marital status, favorite foods/music/movies, and politics.

2. You can also poll people as they leave a restaurant and ask them to rate their experience. Present the findings when they call for your turn. Yeah, good luck with that.

3. If you want to really have fun with people, come up with some questions around math, science, history, or literature (whichever is your strongest subject), and ask adults a couple of questions to see if they are smarter than a (blank) grader. (Hint: You already have all the answers, so you look like a genius.)

WHAT YOU NEED

Pad of paper and pen or pencil. (A clipboard would be ideal.)

Creativity Added

18

The object of this game is to take a basic item and find new and improved uses for it.

Take a clothespin, for example; you can probably come up with a dozen different uses for this household item in under a minute. This holds true with a lot of little things like paper clips, rubber bands, and pens. This activity takes ordinary items and makes them into possible extraordinary products.

HOW TO PLAY

1. Pick any item from your pocket and purse that could possibly have more than one use. Ask the people at the table (or waiting in line) to see how else it could be used.

Award the most innovative idea, but make sure to applaud all the ideas.

2. Take out your cell phone or iPhone and see if you can come up with 50 ways it could be used to better the world—or your world. It's surprising how open younger kids are to new ideas and possibilities. When it comes to creativity, let the little ones participate too. You'll be amazed at what they come up with.

WHAT YOU NEED

Almost any item can be improved or used in a new and creative way.

BONUS

Draw a circle with a dot in the middle on a piece of paper and ask others at the table to re-create an EXACT replica on their paper WITHOUT lifting their pen from the paper. Tell them to work with a partner if possible. It seems impossible not to have a line connecting the circle and dot (which disqualifies a player), but there are several ways to do this. Clever players will use a pen with retractable point, make the circle, and then drag the pen across the paper; use two pens; use two people; use a pencil and erase the line; find a dot already on the paper and draw a circle around it.

Custom Cups

19

Using a Sharpie and scissors, any cup (or plate) can be customized—and become a work of art.

People pay good money to make custom ceramic cups and plates at stores that specialize in those sorts of things. We say, do the same thing with plastic cups and paper plates. Let your imagination run wild as you add a favorite quote to your cup with a marker, or turn your paper plate into a personal expression of your inner artist.

HOW TO PLAY

1. Clear plastic cups are perfect for decorating with a permanent pen. Kids can write

their name, draw a face, make a water line with waves and boats, or customize their cups in any number of different ways. A quick note—most restaurants frown on their guests coloring on their cups and plates, unless they are paper or plastic. In the wrong hands, Sharpies can do more damage in a minute than a plate of spaghetti. Same goes for an inkpad.

2. Paper plates are perfect for turning into masks (with a rubber band for the strap), by cutting them into animal faces or making them into unique (and chic) shapes. The only limit to what's possible is the amount of time and the tools you have to work with.

WHAT YOU NEED

A permanent ink pen (or not), scissors, paper products, and an inkpad.

BONUS

Assuming you carry an inkpad with you in your pocket or purse, almost any item can become a stamp. For example, a potato can be carved into a stamp, same with an apple. You can also take items found on the ground (no, not litter—more like leaves) and make them into cool creations by pressing them on the inkpad and then stamping them on paper.

Dicey

20

Cool games using a pair of dice.

The following activities exemplify just how easy it is to create fun things to do with nothing more than a thing or two found in your pocket or purse. It goes to show how little your fun quotient has to do with what things cost.

HOW TO PLAY

1. **The Great Race.** For this first game, being seated at an Italian restaurant with checkered tablecloth makes it easy. This is a simple race across the table—using whatever you can find as a game piece. If there is no checkered tablecloth at your table (congrats, you eat at better places than us), just use paper to make boxes to count off as

players roll the amount of moves they can take to get across the board. It's that simple. Race from one end to the other.

2. **Board Games.** With a little more effort, you can create your own board game. For example, you can play your own version of Candy Land, where a player gets a piece of candy if they land on the square the sweet is on—or a veggie if they land on the "wrong" square—or is that vice versa? You can invent your own version of *Monopoly* where money is won and lost based upon the rules of each square, or *The Game of Life*, in which players have windfalls or pitfalls based on the roll of the dice. See also Board Games (activity number 9) for more ideas.

3. **Play Ball.** Our favorite game is one we call Roll Dice Baseball (for baseball and stat lovers). You make a score sheet with innings, a place to list your players, and then you keep track of how well they "hit" and "pitch." Determine who is the home team and who is visiting. Then, using your memory or the sports section of a newspaper, each player chooses their team and writes down their lineup and starting pitcher—maybe

even an all-star team. Using the following guide, you roll the dice and determine what the result of your "at bat" was and play the game, keeping score just like regular baseball. Rolling three outs ends that players half of the inning, and runners advance and score with hits and walks. Here are what each roll of the dice means: (Use two dice.) 2 = double; 3 = triple; 4 = homerun; 5 = pop out; 6 = ground out; 7 = walk; 8 = strikeout; 9 = strikeout; 10 = fly out/sacrifice; 11 = single; 12 = double play/out; 13 = check your HGH level.

WHAT YOU NEED

Dice.

Doctor, Doctor

This is a chance to play sick and play doctor—not at the same time, though.

For as long as there has been school, there have been kids pretending to be sick. Now we can turn this into a really fun and informative game. One or more people will pretend to be sick and describe their symptoms (one at a time) until the "doctors" in the room can figure out what's wrong. The first to guess, wins.

HOW TO PLAY

1. For the patient, there are a number of cool ways to fake an injury or illness. Add a little ketchup to your arm and you can have a cut or bullet wound (depending on how

many bottles you use). Use mustard instead, and there are a number of gross things that could be causing you pain. Chew on candy and turn your tongue yellow (jaundice), sprinkle some salt on your dark shirt (dandruff), or just describe some of your symptoms to see which of the "doctors" can guess what you are suffering from.

2. The doctor can then treat the problem with a cast (wrap napkins, tissues, or toilet paper around a wound), prescribe some medicine (a sugar packet), or popsicle sticks and some tape will make a fine splint.

3. If anyone has access to the Internet on their phone (your CrackBerry does have access), this game can be taken to the next level by looking up the answers online. Look up an illness and describe it to the "doctors" to see if they can guess what it is.

4. Another variation is to blindfold the "doctor" to see if they can feel and name the part of the body they are feeling on the other person. Or, see how many body parts they can name by just feeling.

WHAT YOU NEED

Band-Aids, ketchup, toilet paper, sugar, mustard. Perfect ingredients for homemade soup after the game?

BONUS

Many of our parents wanted us to grow up to become doctors, while we yearned to be firefighters or police officers. How about combining the two? (Don't worry, we won't have the kids burning or melting things.) Create a crime scene complete with clues and have family and friends play the roles of witnesses or victims. See if the young detectives can solve the crime "CSI-style".

Family Tree

In this game, you learn a lot of relevant history—your family's history.

In years past (before television and color were invented), family lore and history were passed down from generation to generation through stories. Today, genealogy can be researched online, but it's best to hear how things were from those who lived it. That's why this game is not just fun and fascinating, it's important for instilling a sense of interest (and pride) in the people and places that make up your family tree. You will realize how much history your name has behind it. Obviously, this is intended as a family game, but "family" is a loose term these days, so you could also do this with a group of friends to guess how much you know about their backgrounds.

HOW TO PLAY

1. The easiest way is to draw a tree and work your way from youngest to oldest. Using branches for different arms of the family and leaves to indicate who belongs where, you can get a pretty good picture of your paternal past.

2. See how far a person can go up the family tree by memory.

3. Play it like *Who Wants to Be a Millionaire* and phone a friend (call a relative to help fill in the blanks), use a lifeline to look something up online, or just take a guess.

4. Create teams and play family trivia to see who knows more, using questions like; "Your grandfather was in World War I, true or false?" or "How many miles a day did your mom have to walk to school . . . in the snow?" Make it like a game show and ask a question like, "What relatives did we see on our last vacation?" Each player writes their answers on a sheet of paper and reveals them. See who got the most names right.

5. Or, see how much your family knows about each others' likes and dislikes. Much like they do on *Family Feud*, separately poll each family member with several questions to

find out what the top answers are. Questions range from things they did, things they didn't do but want to, or things related to your family history. Then teams are formed, and the person conducting the poll serves as the host. You play just like the TV version—and feel free to get intimate as the Richard Dawson host does. Maybe you'll learn more about your family than you bargained for. Heyo!

BONUS

If you are at home, use your computer and printer to create a family tree using photos. You can search Google for them, scan old ones in, or take photos of as many family members as possible during the next get-together.

A Few Of My Favorite Things

23

Here are several good games to get to know each others' likes (and dislikes).

We'll break this activity down into the good, the bad, and the ugly because there are several ways to play. For the good, you will get to make a list of all your favorite things, and a wish list of what you want. There is also a game to go along with the things that really bug you (the bad), and players will have a chance to gripe and then get a grip. Lastly, there will be a version of "truth or truth" (there is no dare) where players will reveal things they've done that might surprise people.

HOW TO PLAY

1. "The good" revolves around finding a few of your favorite things. There are a number of ways to do this. First, each person makes a top-10 list of things they would want with them if stranded on a deserted island for a year. This could be favorite foods, people, music, movies, or books. Then others try and guess what's on your list. Each player can only be wrong five times before they are eliminated. The winner is the last person left.

2. Another "good" game involves a "talking stick." In this game, everyone wins because a stick (or ball) is passed from person to person and while holding the stick, it's the job of that participant to say something they are grateful for or something nice about someone else in the room.

3. "The bad" involves a gripe session. First, each player lists the alphabet along the left side of a piece of paper. The object then is to be the first to find something that bugs you beginning with every letter of the alphabet. Extra credit can be given if a player

has a possible solution to a problem.

4. "The ugly" isn't really that bad—unless you've lived a "colorful" life. This activity is designed to reveal some of your secrets in a semi-safe fashion. The first person begins by revealing something daring they did in their past, and other players try to one-up them. Or, if kids are playing and you don't want to have to use "ear muffs," you can simply try and guess something another player has done or not done (been to the Zoo, flown in a helicopter, worked in fast food, and so on).

WHAT YOU NEED

Paper and pen. And openness to sharing your inner thoughts—free your mind, Neo.

Finger Fun

Some simple thumbs-up games involving nothing more than a few of your fingers.

This isn't the first activity in this book to involve digits, but it's one of the few that makes use of your fingers. Here are some really cool "hands-on" games that are both fun and funny.

HOW TO PLAY

1. **Thumb Wrestling.** Thumb wrestling is an old standby (and family favorite) for the bored. You lock fingers with your opponent trying to pin their thumb down with yours. The way to raise the stakes is to do tag-team thumb wrestling. This simply means three

or four players lock their fingers together and team up to pin a person down.

2. **Knock Your Block Off.** Another thumb game involves a little more work, but it will be worth it. Each player will create a hat or helmet for their thumb using a soda top, folded paper, or anything else that can stay on and be knocked off with the flick of a finger. Lock hands together like thumb wrestling, except the object is to knock the opponents thumb cap off.

3. **Rock, Paper, Scissors.** Rock, paper, scissors has been deciding outcomes for years. Each player makes a fist and counts off by tapping their clenched fingers into their palm before revealing their weapon of choice on the count of three—rock (a fist), paper (a flat hand, palm down), or scissors (index and middle finger making a cutting motion). Rock smashes scissors and wins. Paper covers rock, so it comes out on top. Scissors cut paper so it prevails. To make it more fun, you can add other weapons to your arsenal like a gun, grenade, or Spiderman web shooting out of your palm. Or maybe bees, flowers, and ladybugs for the young ones or girls. You get the idea.

4. **Quick Draw.** Slap fights are another way to stay entertained for a few minutes. To play, one player puts both hands palms down in front of them. The second player puts both hands palms up, just under the first player's hands. Player two now will try to surprise player one by slapping his or her hand. Player one tries to get out of the way before getting hit. Players rotate roles and keep score (each hit is a point).

WHAT YOU NEED

Something to make a finger helmet. Quick hands. Strong thumbs.

Fun With Food

Kids, here is your chance to play with your food and not get in trouble.

For many parents it's a constant battle to get kids to eat right. What if we could help you get them to eat just about anything? Okay, that's a stretch, but these games could increase their consumption of several different types of food (the healthy type)—and have fun doing it.

HOW TO PLAY

1. **Taste Test.** You know how parents are always saying, "How do you know you don't like it unless you try it?" Well, here's the chance to make it happen. Blindfold a contes-

tant and offer them three different dishes to see if they can guess what's what—and try a new food or two in the process. Maybe try a new combination of foods like pickles and ice cream. Yeah, we said it.

2. **Mikey Likes It.** Here's a way to take any food item and find out if it would taste better when dipped in chocolate sauce. Order a side of chocolate sauce to do some dipping. The most unusual or grossest combination wins.

3. **Salad Daze.** With food, presentation is a big part of the appeal. Now you can take your food and find new and creative ways to make it a work of art. Cucumbers make great eyes, Roma tomatoes look like a nose, and sunflower seeds look like teeth. Or, just rearrange the things on your plate in an artistic way. The most creative wins.

4. **Ring Toss.** All you need is an order of onion rings and a finger and a new game is born. Players take turns trying to get their onion ring on the other player's finger. Then, when time expires, the person must eat all the rings on their finger the fastest.

5. **Alphabet Soup with French Fries.** French fries can fatten your brain as well as

your waistline when you use them as letters to spell out words and phrases.

6. **Fear Factor.** The game is simple—see who will eat the grossest thing, or which player can eat the grossest thing the fastest. Or figure out the oddest food combinations. (Adults will want to oversee this one to make sure nothing dangerous is consumed and to ask if anyone has allergies to certain types of food first.)

7. **Stuff Your Face.** Sure, it's bad manners to talk with your mouth full and stuff your face. But if it's part of a game to see who has the biggest mouth . . . This is the "Frank The Tank" drinking and eating contest, but instead of suds we recommend milk.

9. **Mr. Potato Head.** If you take an ordinary potato and start sticking things in it you have a hot kid's toy. (When we say hot, we mean it.) Decorate your baked potato any way you want using whatever you can find.

WHAT YOU NEED

A restaurant. Maybe even one with a diverse menu.

Guessing Games

26

Everyone likes to guess correctly and get a pat on the back. This is their chance.

There are dozens of different ways to encourage kids (and adults) to test their intellect and intuition in a good guessing game. Do you have any idea what one or two of these games are? Gotcha.

HOW TO PLAY

1. **Numbers.** Ask a person to try and guess the number of chairs in a restaurant, CDs in a case, people in a room, or how many gumballs are in the vending machine. The closest to the right number wins. (You'll have to count the gumballs first. Good luck.)

2. **People.** Each person is given the name of a famous person (sports, politics, movies), and then each player asks each other yes or no questions to figure each person's hidden identity. Another way to do it is to write a famous figure's name on a napkin or sticky note and attach it to the back of a player's shirt so the wearer can't see the name on the piece of paper. Now others give that player clues about who they're supposed to be, and each player has to guess their own hidden identity. Or, write famous names on slips of paper and put them in a hat. Each person gets a turn to grab a random name and give hints to see if the others can guess who it is.

3. **Lies.** On a napkin, sheet of paper, sticky note, or index card, write three things about yourself that another might not easily know—but make one of them not true. For example, you can write: 1.) I like math 2.) I'm afraid of tiny dogs 3.) I like Hannah Montana. Others try to figure which of the three are not true. This is an easy one for others to guess about me.

4. **Origins.** Look at a menu and see if anyone knows the origins of the dish (french fries

are indeed from France, but turkey sandwiches did not originate in Turkey). Google is a good way to check these using a handheld device with access to the Internet. Kids can turn the tables on adults by asking questions or facts and figures about what they are into to see if the "old folks" know anything about what is hip and new. Chances are their parents will be playing at a fourth-grade level. It probably should be true or false in nature to give the old geezers a fighting chance. Ah, but the parents can return the favor by playing what (or who) came first. Kids could do this to adults, too. The game is simple: ask participants which came first—iTunes or Google, the automobile or the telephone, Thomas Jefferson or Abe Lincoln, Hawaii or Alaska?

WHAT YOU NEED

Nothing. Well, maybe a good memory.

Hangin' Around

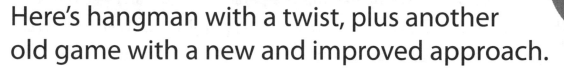

27

Here's hangman with a twist, plus another old game with a new and improved approach.

You can play the traditional hangman method or add a few twists to make it more interactive. Raise the stakes by playing for spare change in your pocket or a piece or candy or gum. It's amazing how into it kids will get when a simple "tic tac" or dime is on the line.

HOW TO PLAY

1. **Hangman.** The traditional game has entertained families for years. Pick a word, draw blank lines for each letter of the word, players guess at the letters, you draw body

parts for each incorrect guess . . . you get it. Try picking a word related to where you are, what you're doing, or who you're with, maybe even whole sentences. We thought it would be fun to raise the stakes by making the person who doesn't get the word right have to hang on to something for half an hour. You can also play *Wheel of Fortune* style and after each letter, the guesser has three seconds to solve. Move on to the next person if they don't guess correctly. The person with the most puzzles solved wins.

2. **Tic Tac Toe, Toe, Toe.** We are assuming everyone knows how to play tic-tac-toe. What makes it more fun is to add more boxes. With more squares, your strategy changes. Try it, you'll like it.

WHAT YOU NEED

Paper and pencils.

Heads Up

Here are some coin games to pass the time—and possibly pass the buck.

Heads or tails? There could be a lot riding on your answer—especially when you play our way. Most of us have loose change in our pocket or purse. Even though a lot of us are "pinching pennies" these days, it still can be a burden to carry around coins. Here is your chance to have some fun and lighten your load. Besides, two bits will mean a lot more to a kid when they win it fair and square in one of the following activities.

HOW TO PLAY

1. **Heads You Win.** This one is so simple. The person who correctly guesses whether

the coin will land on heads or tails when flipped (or falls off the table) wins the coin. If there is a tie, the person who comes closest to guessing the year the coin was issued wins the coin. The person at the table with the most money at the end wins the game or keeps their coins.

2. **Big Numbers.** Another coin game can be a contest of guessing if the next coin the "dealer" pulls out of his or her pocket is larger or smaller than the previous one. You begin by placing a coin on the table. If it's a quarter, a player would probably guess the next coin will be smaller (unless you're pinching silver dollars these days). If it's a penny, the chances are the next one would be larger. This is good for young kids who will start to learn the denominations of each type of coin.

3. **Dead Presidents.** If you want to raise the stakes, use big bills. The contest can be a memory game. Let players look at a bill for a few seconds and then quiz them on what they can recall seeing—the year, the president on the front, the denomination, the last four serial numbers, and so on. Winner takes all—or as much as you let them.

4. **Shell Game.** The old shell game is always fun for kids. Place a coin under a coffee cup and move the cups around. The first one to find the correct cup with the coin underneath, keeps the coin. Or pass the cups on to the correct guesser, and so on.

5. **Pitching Pennies . . . and Quarters.** Pitching pennies was once a favorite among kids (and dock workers). It's simple—each player stands a few feet from a wall and tries to pitch, flick, or slide his or her coin the closest to the wall. The closest wins both coins.

WHAT YOU NEED

Silver (and copper) coins.

Hoop Dreams

29

A series of sports games using folded or wadded-up paper.

Here are a few competitive games that will delight the kids and drive (a few) parents nuts. They will help with kid's hand-eye coordination and help you figure out which sports agent's phone number to keep handy. Just for the record, we both came from very normal, suburban families with parents who definitely set boundaries, but . . . enjoy.

HOW TO PLAY

1. **Spit Ball.** There are many clever ways to emulate Olympic events, but we're pretty

sure a spitball contest isn't one of them. This game is played by wadding up a small piece of paper in your mouth to form a small ball. This slobbery, round projectile is then loaded into your straw. Time to let the spit-cathalon begin! By blowing hard, the wet ball is shot into the air. You can play for accuracy and distance, or you can guess how long it will be before Mom or Dad puts an end to this game. Or how long it will take you to get escorted to the front door of Carl's Jr. (Note: You can do many of the same things simply by blowing the protective wrapper from your straw.)

2. **Dodge Ball.** Getting drilled by one of those red balls in grade school hurts. The worst thing that can happen by being hit by a wadded-up piece of paper is . . . nothing. But when your team is counting on you *not* to get hit so you can win in Dodge Ball, then it stings—for a different reason. The other game that can be played is Smear the Fear (yes, we reworded it). This means whoever is holding the ball can be gang tackled—or worse.

3. **Paper Lions.** By folding a piece of paper into a small triangular shape you have cre-

ated your "football." Next, you will be "kicking" your "ball" by steadying it on the table with a single finger on one hand and flicking with a finger from your other hand. The object of the game is to get a goal—a field goal—by launching it through the uprights (another person's hands with the thumbs touching and index fingers pointing up).

5. **Volleyball.** Keep the paper ball in the air. See how many hits in a row you can keep the ball in the air—as a group or just one person at a time. Or keep the ball in the air for a timed amount. Then the next team has to beat your time. Or make a net with drinks or the salt and pepper shakers at your table and hit the ball back and forth over the net. (This one can get messy.)

6. **Basketball.** The easiest way to play is to see who can sink as many of their paper basketballs into a trash can. You can give more points for distance or difficulty, or score for consistency. At a restaurant, make a hoop with your hands. Players shoot from all spots around the table. Or spin a coin at the table and catch the spinning coin with two fingers and without readjusting, shoot from the caught spot into the hoop hands.

7. **Golf.** Use silverware from the table as clubs and see how many "strokes" it take to get from one side of the table to the "hole" on the other side. Set up as many obstacles in the middle as you want. Use a coin or wad of paper as your golf ball. You may even get in a full 18 holes if your waiter is slow as molasses. Usually it's nine and dine.

8. **Paper Airplanes.** Contests for distance, design, flight time. We thought we would end with something safe. Just make sure to wear safety goggles. Let your conditions be your guide to the rules of flight—go with the wind for distance; against the wind for number of loop-de-loops; most colorful, etc. You can even play paper airplane golf to see how many throws it takes you to get from one spot to the next "airport."

WHAT YOU NEED

Paper, coins, silverware—sounds like the NY Mercantile Stock Exchange.

Huh?

Invent your own language and phrases.

Parents and kids have had a hard time communicating as long as there have been toddlers and teenagers. So we thought, let's make it even harder. Just kidding. We have found that kids love inventing their own language—hoping their parents don't get the decoder card. So let's just go with it.

HOW TO PLAY

1. An easy way to play is to have everyone figure out what their name is backward. This is a lot of fun and gets things going. For the rest of the night, people must use your backward name. If they slip up, they are out (or is that "tuo"?).

2. When Frankie Smith and Snoop Dogg started adding IZZLE to the end of words to create their own language ("Fo schizzle my nizzle") they opened the door for a lot of new "languages" to be born. Whether it's called Pig Latin or Urban Speak, have fun with making up your own dialect.

3. Another way to play is everyone has to speak in rhymes. The first one that forgets, or gets stuck, is out. (Or they must "rap" what they want to say for a day. Yes way!)

4. Create your own sign language using motions and hand signals—kind of like a catcher giving signs to a pitcher. Make up hand signals like touching your nose to ask someone to pass the butter. Or tug on your earlobe to ask to be excused from the table. These signs can be carried over a few days, weeks, or a lifetime if you're really lucky.

WHAT YOU NEED

Maybe a pencil to find out how words are pronounced backwards phonetically. And paper to keep track of your hand signals.

It's In The Bag

This is a memory game using actual objects from your pocket or purse.

Here's a chance for us to see who you really are. Isn't who you are revealed by what you carry in your purse? Wallets for men? Here's a chance to clean out your purse or wallet and entertain your group all at the same time. Just make sure what you pull out isn't a surprise to you too!

HOW TO PLAY

1. Put several random items on the table or pass them around—keys, a wallet, phone, watch—and then put them in a bag (or a hat, box, under the table) and see who can

remember exactly what they saw.

2. Or, remove one item from the table to see if anyone can figure out what's missing.

3. Hide a small item somewhere on the table and see who can find it first.

4. Another good memory game is to gather a few people in a circle and start with a short phrase or word based on a theme. The next person must repeat the first phrase or word and add one of their own. As you go around the room, each person must remember and recite all the phrases that came before. If they fail, they are eliminated.

WHAT YOU NEED

A hat or bag. Photographic memory. Maybe a thesaurus too?

Jack And Jill

32

Just playing jacks is fun; but our way is even better.

Jacks is a game of skill and agility, and it can be one of profitability too. Jacks is traditionally played by bouncing a ball to see how many pieces a player can pick up before catching the same ball before it hits the ground. What if you played with coins or candy instead—and the player gets to keep what they can pick up? Cool, eh? That's how we play and kids are all of a sudden more motivated, focused, and coordinated than ever.

HOW TO PLAY

1. Start with a bouncy ball. (If you don't have a ball, used a wadded-up piece of paper,

throw it in the air and catch it instead of bouncing it.) The goal is to grab what you can while the ball is in the air. If the ball hits the ground, you get nothing. If you are able to hang onto what you scooped up and catch your ball, then that's what you keep. You then get another turn—and keep going until you miss. Or you can pass and keep what you already have scooped up. At the end of the game, you add up what each player has—in coins or candy—and see who has the most.

2. For the really young players, an adult can be the designated "catcher" while the kids are responsible for grabbing the goodies. For this team event, you'll need at least two adults and two kids.

WHAT YOU NEED

A bouncing ball or paper wad, coins, and candy.

King Of The Circle

33

The object of the game is to be the last one standing in the circle.

This game could be called Lord of the Ring because the object of the game is to be the last one left standing inside the ring that has been marked off with chalk or string. Maybe this would be a good time to issue the warning that this could involve some real rough-housing, but it can also be good clean (non-contact) fun. Read on and see how.

HOW TO PLAY

1. **The Ring.** First, draw a circle on the ground with chalk and everyone gets inside. When the whistle blows (an adult screams "go") each player has to run around. The

goal is to be the last one left standing inside the circle (or designated area). Of course, you can win by sheer force by pushing the other players outside the circle (and this is our preference). Last man standing wins—like the *Thunderdome*. One way to "entice" players to leave the circle is to offer incentives like candy or coins. You can also add black holes by drawing smaller circles inside the big one. To get the numbers down yell "freeze." Any player standing in a black hole, is out. Or, when they are frozen, you ask a trivia question. Anyone who gets it right, stays. Anyone who misses it . . .

2. **Hands On.** A totally different game (and one where we didn't know where to stick it) could be called "Hand over Fist." We first learned this game in Little League (and backyard wiffle-ball tournaments) where we couldn't decide which team bats first. We would throw a bat in the air. The captain from one team would catch it, and then the other player would put their hand around the bat on top of the first person's hand. Then, turn by turn (and hand by hand), they would reach the top of the bat. The last person who could fit their hand on the bat, won. You could play this same game with a

stick or a candy cane—winner eats it (the candy cane).

3. **Tug of War.** Using T-shirts tied together (or rope, if you have it) a good ole game of Tug of War can be a good way to bring a family together (or tear it apart).

4. **Pirate's Booty.** To begin, mark off (on the ground with chalk or string) the outline of two pirate ships. Then, the pirates (your kids and their friends) pick their ship. Once there is an equal number of "pirates" per ship, each ship is given the same amount of treasure (coins, keys, and other small items.) The goal is to try to get rid of your booty before the other ship does. The catch is, you can (and should) toss your stuff onto their ship to make it harder for them to lighten their load—see Battleground.

5. **Capture the Flag.** Capture the other team's treasure before they capture yours—see Battleground.

WHAT YOU NEED

Chalk, rope, coins.

Knot Exactly

34

Have you ever wanted to tie up your mother, brother, or best friend? Now you can.

This game can be played with rope, string, or your shoelaces. Try to tie someone up to see if they can free themselves. We realize that sounds a little scary—for the person being tied up. How about creating the impossible knot to see if the kids can untie it in under five minutes. You just have to hope they don't create the impossible knot when they tie you up.

HOW TO PLAY

1. **Knot Me.** This game is best played by two teams. One team uses rope, shoelaces (or

tape) to tie up (and down) a player on the opposing team, and vice versa. Then it's a race to see who can free their tied-up teammate first.

2. **Houdini.** Or a group can gang up on one person and tie them up. The goal is to get unshackled before time runs out.

3. **Knot Today.** Tie a knot in a rope or shoelace and see if the other person can untie it. Race against the clock, or each other, or your parent.

4. **Not Without My Mummy.** Using rolls of toilet paper (stay with us), each team tries to be the first to wrap up a team member. No skin showing, only the eyes.

WHAT YOU NEED

Shoelaces, string, rope or tape, toilet paper—and some scissors, just in case. Note: All these games might require adult supervision.

Last Laugh

35

The goal is to make the other person laugh without touching them.

Using funny faces, clean jokes, and being generally silly (but no touching), you must make other people laugh. To make the game more interesting—and messy—the audience will fill their mouths with water. Your goal is to make them laugh so much they involuntarily spit out their water.

HOW TO PLAY

1. The first way to play is to have a couple of comedians trying to be the first to make one person laugh out loud. Next step is to add water into the equation. Try to make

your audience laugh hard enough to spit out their mouthful of water. Or, you can have the entire audience fill their mouths with water. If the "comedian" can make just one laugh, he or she wins. Or the last one not laughing wins, and they get to be the next joke teller. (Tip—a good knock-knock joke will always get someone with their mouthful of water to "spill.")

WHAT YOU NEED

Water. Some good jokes or funny faces.

Last Straw

36

These are some games using little more than a couple of straws—and a lot of hot air.

Call us blowhards if you must, but we believe there's a lot you can do with a plastic tube and a couple of props. No we're not talking about the ER. Just a way to get an ice cream headache without the ice cream, and still feel good about it.

HOW TO PLAY

1. Of course the easiest way to play with your straw is to see who can blow the outside wrapper the farthest.

2. You can also see how far you can blow a packet of sugar, pasta, or a Cheerio off the

end of a straw. Better yet, challenge others at your table to see who can move their game piece across the table (and a finish line) the fastest.

3. An oldie but goodie is to use your straw (and only your straw) to get all the water from one glass into another. Do this by sucking water into your straw and then "capping" it with your finger to hold it in while you transfer it from one cup to another.

4. Try to assemble a bunch of straws together and see how many you can put together and still get a drink out of your cup. Our record is 17.

WHAT YOU NEED

Straws, sugar packets, small objects.

BONUS

Use straws to create a crazy and cool new hairdo for your sister. Use the straws as barrettes to hold hair in place—and in places it probably wasn't meant to be.

Liar's Club

37

Who is lying and who is telling the truth—which is which?

Players roll dice and try to figure out how many of the same number are on the table (with players concealing their dice from others). The object of these games is to try and figure out who is the best at fibbing. Remember, truth is stranger than fiction so this is harder than it sounds.

HOW TO PLAY

1. **Liar's Dice.** Each player has 3 to 5 dice, and everyone rolls at once, concealing their roll from the other players. The first person tries to guess how many of the dice are a

certain number. For example, player 1 guesses 5 out of all the dice are 3s. Then player 2 has to beat player 1 by guessing higher than 5 threes: like 5 fours, 5 fives, 5 sixes, 6 ones, 6 twos, etc. Players continue guessing and lying around the circle until someone is called out as a LIAR. When a player calls someone else a LIAR, everyone reveals their dice. Then everyone counts the number of dice the person called out as a LIAR originally guessed. As long as there are at least the same or more of their guessed number, the person called out as a LIAR wins that round, and the person who called them a LIAR loses a dice. If the person called out as a LIAR has overestimated the number of dice, then that person (the LIAR) loses a dice. The game continues until everyone loses their dice but one person. You can add to the game by considering 1s are wild.

2. Another "truth or dare" game is to see who has the best poker face. Try and bluff the other players with what you have in your hand—which could be anything. Or, you can use cards, and try to bluff people by saying, for example, that you have four red cards or three aces. Then you bet (with pennies or sugar packets). You can do the same with

money. Or you can play with dollar bills by using the serial numbers. You can claim you have four 4s or a pair of . . .

WHAT YOU NEED

Lots of dice. A good imagination.

Long Jump

A contest to see who can jump the farthest.

What child doesn't like a challenge? What kid wouldn't "jump" at the chance to try to outdistance another in a leaping contest? Exactly. The Long Jump is perfect for kids (and adults) who are bored while stuck in line or waiting for a table at a restaurant. This can be played anywhere, anytime—including indoors.

HOW TO PLAY

1. Mark the starting point on the ground with objects like a set of keys or a cell phone. (Optional: Use chalk or string to form a starting line.)

2. Make a second line a foot or so away. Each child gets a chance to jump from one line to the other. Those who make it advance to the next level.

3. You keep moving the line farther away until a record is set and you have a winner.

4. Or, make it an endurance test. Parents can also play jumping on only one leg.

5. Have a contest to see who can stand on one leg the longest.

WHAT YOU NEED

Weighted objects to mark off the jump. Chalk or string (optional) for actual long-jump lines.

Mind Reader

This takes "What are you thinking?" and turns it into a game.

It's hard to believe that you can actually make an activity out of "I'm thinking of a number from one to 100," but it's possible.

HOW TO PLAY

1. This is one of the oldest games in the book. The easiest way to play "guess what I'm thinking" is to begin by writing down a number from one to 100 on a piece of paper. Then, participants have to guess what that number is. The closest, wins. (The paper serves as proof.)

2. Another way to play is to pick a famous person (or an item in the room) and see who can guess who (or what) you're thinking of using clues. They only get three guesses, but can ask an unlimited number of clue questions. (Good yes or no questions include: Do you eat it? Is it big? Is it in this room?)

WHAT YOU NEED

Paper, pen, and patience.

Movie Magic

Make a movie using your camera phone (or video camera) and a computer.

This one came from a television commercial. In the ad a young boy takes pictures of his toy animals attacking each other and then imports the photos into his computer, adds a soundtrack, and voilá, a movie is made. If your kids carry around their toys (okay, so they aren't in your pocket or purse, but a backpack is close enough), then this could work with cars, dolls, or just about anything else—like people.

HOW TO PLAY

1. You can use your toys to act, direct, and produce your own mini movie. This can

be done by taking snapshots of scenes and then putting them all together with some photo software to create a movie.

2. Think about the possibilities with this medium. With the right camera (video or still) and some props, a couple of actors (your friends and family) you can star in your own television drama, reality show, or comedy.

BONUS

You can also create a "play" so you can do these without a video camera.

WHAT YOU NEED

Laptop, camera, and some props.

Musical Menus

41

It's the same as musical chairs, only using menus instead.

The premise behind musical chairs (which is a very fun game to play) is to have fewer chairs than people. When the music starts (or people begin by clapping), participants circle the chairs until the leader yells sit. Since there aren't enough chairs for everyone, one person will be left standing—and out of the game. You keep playing (and removing chairs) until there is one winner. The following games are variations on this theme.

HOW TO PLAY

1. **Musical Menus.** The game begins with one less menu than people seated at the ta-

ble. When the music starts (a person can sing or hum a tune), begin passing the menus from person to person. When the "music" stops, the person left without a menu is eliminated. You then pull another menu and continue until there is only one left.

2. **Musical Phones.** If you get bored with Musical Menus, try musical phones. Except instead of passing the phones around, see who can create the coolest song using the keypad tones.

3. **The Elimination Game.** Gather everyone into a circle. On the ground in front of each person is a sheet of paper with the instructions and awards on them—including one or two that say "You are eliminated." Like "Musical Chairs", everyone moves in a circle until the leader yells "stop." The players get whatever is coming to them based on the paper in front of them.

4. **Duck, Duck, Goose.** In a traditional game of "Duck, Duck, Goose," a player taps each seated player on the head saying "duck" until someone is chosen by saying "Goose." That player (the Goose) must chase and tag the player to get out of being "it." And so it

goes. Our version is similar, but instead of everyone *sitting* around the circle, everyone stands. The leader then walks around the circle trying to tap each person while each player "ducks" (or bobs and weaves) to avoid being tagged. If the person can't get out of the way, then they are "it" and must chase and tag another.

WHAT YOU NEED

Menus, cell phones, paper, and pens.

Name That Tune

42

This game is exactly what it sounds like—
a chance to show off your musical prowess.

Can you name a song in one or two notes? Are you good with guessing one-liners from films? Then you will love these games. Using your iPod, a laptop, cell phone, or just the piped in music wherever you are, you can entertain a group for a few minutes or more. Here's how . . .

HOW TO PLAY

1. **Name That Tune.** You are going to do the iPod shuffle. Play a song for a person (but don't let them see the screen) to see if they can guess who it is. You can give clues

if you want, or just give them until the song is over to get it right. But the best way to play is to see which player can guess a song just by hearing the first few seconds of it. Keep track of who got it right, and the one with the most is dubbed the musical genius. To get others involved, you can give out extra points for whoever can name the artist, album, and other tidbits in addition to naming the tune. Try giving out 5 points for the first to name the tune and 1 point for every tidbit after. That may let the genius let someone else answer first so he can show off by getting points for the tidbits. Then its win-win for everyone.

2. **Name That Movie.** "Make my day" and "May the force be with you" and "I'll be back" are classic movie lines. This game is simple. One player tries to stump the others by picking a well-known phrase from a movie and saying it aloud to see who can guess either the film it's from, the film star who said it, or both.

3. **Name That Person**. "One step for man . . ." and "Ask not what your country can do for you . . ." and "I had a dream . . ." and "You're my boy, Blue . . ." are a part of our his-

tory. These classic quotes can be started by the leader, and players must either finish them or guess who said what.

WHAT YOU NEED

iPod. Hours in front of the movie screen.

Napkin Dreams

43

Take an ordinary napkin and turn it into a work of art or the plans for the future.

Many businesses have been launched with nothing more than some sketches on a napkin. Some of the easiest art projects involve nothing more than tissue paper and a pair of scissors. With the activities below, you can do both—create a business plan or a beautiful work of art.

HOW TO PLAY

1. **Cut Up.** We'll begin with the easiest activity first. A folded (paper) napkin can become a garland in a matter of minutes with a pair of scissors. Kids can make the clas-

sics: snowflakes, hearts, or figures holding hands. With a little experimentation, who knows what kind of creation will come next.

Cut-Up BONUS: After you and the kids cut out a few hundred snowflakes, use fishing line and tape to hang them from the ceiling to create a winter wonderland.

2. **Blue Prints.** You can take the same anything-goes "blueprint" concept and apply it to any building—the ultimate classroom, vacation home, or playroom. For this next activity, creativity is also needed, but in a completely different way. Depending on the age of the participants, there are several ways to go. First, you can ask kids to draw their ideal room (blueprint style) on a napkin. Allow them to create a space where anything goes. Do they want a petting zoo? Cool. How about a basketball court? Nice. A movie theater? No problem. Or, if you want it more reality-based, rearrange their furniture and see if another configuration may make more sense. Have them draw a blueprint of their room, or house, or neighborhood. Keep expanding to see how far they can go.

3. **Business Plan.** Have the kids sketch the basics of a business they would want to own if they could. What would they call it, what would they sell, what would it look like, what would their logo be. Would they have a fleet of private planes, limos, trucks? Would they want to do something to save the world? What would that look like?

WHAT YOU NEED

Napkins, pens, scissors.

Nature Lover

44

Kids create their own bracelet using tape (sticky side out) and things found in nature.

Talk about going green. This activity is about as green as it gets—and it's good fun, too. This can be a game—see which person can complete their bracelet the fastest or the best—or it can be a teaching tool, explaining a little about the things collected from outside. It's also an art project, with the right combination of twigs, leaves, bugs, and other things gathered and glued to their wrists, kids can make a statement.

HOW TO PLAY

1. It all begins with tape wrapped around the wrist with the sticky side out. The wider

the better. The rest is simple, kids go outside to create their own unique bracelets using items found in nature. Be aware, boys may go for the bugs and girls might grab flowers—or vice versa.

2. Of course, this could be the perfect way to get rid of a lot of the loose little things at the bottom of your purse. Put those buttons, business cards, and other bizarre stuff for which you have no idea what it is or does on the table and let the kids go to town.

WHAT YOU NEED

Tape. Book of non-poisonous plants.

The Newlywed Game (Family Style)

45

Do we really know anyone? We are about to find out.

How well do we really know our family? We're about to find out. How much do you *want* to know? Scary, eh?

HOW TO PLAY

1. This is played similarly to the old *Newlywed Game*. One person is questioned about a few of their favorite things while the other player is out of earshot. After answering

all the questions, bring them back together and ask the person who left what they thought the answer was that their partner gave. Give points for correct guesses. Then they switch places.

2. Ask both people separately the same set of questions about their likes and dislikes. Bring them back together and now the fun begins. See how well they know each other by having them guess what the other said was their favorite food, color, music, movie, and other preferences. You can give points to each team if you are divided into pairs.

3. Mix it up and play *Survivor* style and have someone leave the table. Proceed to ask all the other table members what they think the subject will answer to specific questions you have made up. Bring the subject back and ask him/her the questions. See how everyone did and add up points for correct guesses.

WHAT YOU NEED

Paper and pens. No whoopee.

Oprah

Create your own television talk show and interview each other.

One of our favorite *Seinfeld* episodes is when Kramer re-creates the *The Merv Griffin Show* in his apartment. That got us thinking—what if you put together your own *Oprah* or *Ellen* show. One person is the host, another the guest, and the rest are the audience. There are a lot of ways to make this really fun for all.

HOW TO PLAY

Just like your favorite talk show, replicate a set using a couple of chairs, a table, and any other props that will make it appear real. You can even do a stand-up routine of funny things about your family or friends (or current events) to open the show. Then have a question-and-answer session with your guests, who can be themselves or pretend to be a famous celebrities or well-known experts in their field. The topics can be anything you want them to be from things you learned in school to a full-blown talent show.

WHAT YOU NEED

A camera if you want to record it; nothing if you just want to have some spontaneous fun.

Parent Trap

This is a chance to trade places with your kids—for a few minutes.

What kid hasn't said, "You just don't understand, Mom." What parent hasn't wanted to say, "You think being a parent is easy? You should try it sometime." Well, here is a chance for parents to trade places with their kids for a while.

HOW TO PLAY

1. Parents, it's time for you to get in touch with your inner child. You can either play the role of the spoiled brat to give kids a taste of their own medicine, or you can show them an example of what a good kid you were when you were young (and see if they

buy it). Depending on the age of the child you are swapping roles with, you can really have fun with this by doing some of the same things they do.

2. Kids grow up too fast, and this will be proof of that. Allow your kids to have some of the perks an adult would get as well as some of the responsibilities. You can even take this to extremes and bring them to work with you one day so they can see what you deal with.

3. You can even switch clothing if you have the guts for it (no pun intended). Have the kids make dinner while you clown around or finish their homework. Or have them clear the table, do the dishes, check the Internet and watch SportsCenter while you get on jammies and brush your teeth for bed. Maybe even switch beds to sleep in. That is if you don't mind sleeping on the plastic-sheet-covered bed.

WHAT YOU NEED

Nerves of steel.

Pass It On

48

The object off this activity is to take a scribble and create a work of art.

Creating art is fun but sometimes you don't know where or how to start that next masterpiece. This game will allow everyone to bring out the Van Gogh in themselves. It is interesting to see what you can create together, or how each person sees something different in a picture, or how each person sees a different potential in a drawing.

HOW TO PLAY

1. **Face Time.** Start by drawing a circle and keep passing the paper along to people until you finish the face—or the entire body if you have time. Keep it going around

the table, or around the room, and each person adds one facial feature at a time and then passes it on. You can even ask strangers to make their mark on it. It's best to start with the head and allow the next person to add one thing only (an eye, nose, mouth, ear, or some hair).

2. **Scribble Me This.** This one starts with a scribble (usually contributed by a child), and then the adult must finish the masterpiece by turning it into something recognizable. Or, you can pass it around and see what happens as the next person adds to it.

3. **Cloud Cover.** Someone draws a cloud or a scribble—do not add anything to it. Pass the drawing around the table and everyone tells what they see in the drawing. Or what it could be made into. Remember the ink-drawing psychology test? Don't forget, you can answer "cookies" for everything.

WHAT YOU NEED

Crayons, markers, and paper.

Pencil Pusher

49

These are races and games played with pencils or pens.

Remember junior high school and playing tank wars on paper? Or car races? Well, not if you're only nine years old right now. That's why we'll show you how to have a race without a driver's license, or how to stage a tank war with no real tanks. Tank you very much.

HOW TO PLAY

1. On a piece of paper, draw starting and finishing lines for your race. (You can draw an entire racetrack if you like.) Then, you will draw a small race car at the starting line.

(We usually use the perspective of looking down on the cars. It's faster and easier to draw this way, and it makes more sense.) Now that you are ready to race, put your pencil (or pen) on your car and place your index finger on the top of the pencil's eraser. Start the race by flicking (pushing down and out) your pencil to see how far the tip goes. Mark the spot where the line your pencil made ends. This is where you will place the point of your pencil to begin your next turn. You then proceed to make your way down (or around) the track until crossing the finish line.

2. Another version of this game is a battle. Draw a plane, helicopter, tank, ship, or soldiers, and then you "shoot" at each other's army by flicking your pencil (just like in game number one). When you hit something you cross it off. (You can determine how many direct hits it takes to sink a ship or crash a plane.) The person who eliminates the "enemy" first, wins.

3. Draw a grid of dots only—for example, 20 dots to a line, and 20 lines—a bunch of small boxes with no sides, only dots at the corners. In turn, each player draws a side to

one box, one dot-to-dot at a time. If your side completes the fourth side to the box, fill in that box with your color or initials, and go again. Keep drawing boxes until the entire grid is filled with boxes and initials. Count up who has the most boxes and they win.

WHAT YOU NEED

Pencil or pen, and paper.

Perspective

50

This is about seeing the small stuff to get the big picture—and change your perspective.

Many of us are creatures of habit. We listen to the same radio stations, watch the same news programs, take the same route to work or school, and eat at familiar places. Sometimes it's a good thing to shake up our lives a little. Here's how.

HOW TO PLAY

1. Create a viewfinder by cutting a small square in the middle of a piece of paper. Have people quickly describe what they see around them. Then have them look only through the little square for a few minutes and ask them what they see. Many times

their perspective changes when forced to zoom in on things.

2. Give kids a chance to see what it would be like to be blind or deaf (or both—boy, that sounds mean, doesn't it?). Using a blindfold or by putting cotton in their ears or headphones on their ears, make them function for a few minutes without the aid of sight and/or sound so they have a greater appreciation for those who lack these senses.

3. Our favorite exercise is to have everyone switch hands for an hour. They must write, eat, and do everything with their non-writing hand. You can assign participants a sport to play with their opposite hand. Make them write or draw something. Or just force them to function with only one hand. Tie the other one behind their back or to their side if you have to. Use your knot-tying skills from Knot Exactly.

WHAT YOU NEED

Paper, scissors, blindfold, cotton balls, or headphones.

Pile It On

The object is to create a structure using some of the things lying around the room.

You've seen stuff piled a mile high in their room, now let's have a little fun with it. This is a timed activity to see who can create the tallest "tower" on top of a table using ordinary objects within reach. The contest can be judged on height, structural integrity, originality, creativity—or just who built the biggest pile of junk the fastest.

HOW TO PLAY

1. Have kids gather up things to create a tower of objects. You can do this anywhere—their room, the living room, a restaurant. What you will stack will depend on your

location. At a restaurant, we suggest cups, salt and pepper shakers, sugar packet holders, ketchup bottles—whatever is on the table. If items are limited, add from your pocket or purse. Or see who can pile up all the items the fastest.

2. If you are at home, pile the pillows and blankets as high as you can. It's always fun to then destroy the castle after you see how tall you can build it. Sometimes that's actually the most fun part.

WHAT YOU NEED

A lot of stackable stuff.

Pump It Up

Some great games using balloons.

The subtitle says it all.

HOW TO PLAY

1. Using a rolled up newspaper, play a little balloon baseball or balloon hockey. Or, find a hedge and play balloon volleyball.

2. Tape balloons to the legs of all the players and mark off an area that the participants must remain within, and then let them loose to try and flatten each other's balloons by stomping on them. When your balloon bursts, you are out of the game. The last person with a balloon intact wins.

3. Throw a balloon in the air and see how many people and how many times you can touch it before it hits the ground.

4. Give everyone a balloon and see who can blow theirs up the biggest (without popping). Hold a separate contest for the fastest.

5. You can fill your balloons with water and raise the stakes. Now an ordinary game of catch takes on a whole new dynamic with a balloon filled with water. For instance, you can pass your water balloon back and forth to see how many times you can go before dropping it. Keep track and see if anyone else can beat your record. You can also have a shot-put contest to see who can fling their water balloon the farthest. You can blindfold the player with the water balloon and play high stakes Marco Polo. (They hurl a water balloon at your voice.) Mom's love this version.

WHAT YOU NEED

Balloons. Water faucet.

Rave Reviews

This is a chance to review everything from friends and food, to movies and music.

Everyone is a critic—and this activity will prove it.

HOW TO PLAY

1. The easiest way to play is to simply review where you are and what you are doing. How would you rate the restaurant you are dining in? The town you are visiting on vacation? The activity you are engaged in? Come up with your own rating system. Hearts means you love it, stars mean it's awesome, and an "X" means it stinks.

2. What about reviewing people you know? Make a list running down the left side of

the page of the people you want to review. Then put a circle next to each name. Now the fun begins. You can simply put a plus sign in the circle if the person is positive and pleasant to be around or a minus sign if they are not. Or, you can fill in the face. If you really like the person, put a happy face. If they are just okay, make their mouth a straight line. If they make you crazy, make their mouth a squiggly line. If they make you sad or mad, give them an upside down smile (a frown). Put a hat on the heads of the happy faces to remind you which were your "best" friends. (Now let your parents score the same people. Yikes!)

3. You can use stickers and go around the room and put stickers on the people you really like. Kids can decide which of their toys is best by the number of stickers they choose to put on them.

WHAT YOU NEED

Paper and pens; stickers are an option.

Scrappy

You can do a lot with a newspaper, magazine, or a catalog.

Many times when you're out and about, you'll see free magazines, newspapers, and catalogs there for the taking. Do it, because when combining these exercises with a couple of complimentary publications, a pair of scissors, and some glue, you can really have fun.

HOW TO PLAY

1. **Puzzled.** For this activity, thicker is better. What you will do is cut up an ad or picture from a magazine (if possible, first glue it to cardboard) and then cut it up into

puzzle pieces. See if the contestants can complete the puzzle in under a set number of minutes. You can also use a drawing to create a puzzle by cutting it up.

2. **Guess What I Am?** Take a photo, illustration, or an ad from a magazine and either cut it into four pieces or fold it so only a portion shows. Ask players to guess what they are looking at. You can reveal a little more each time if they are having trouble.

4. **Scrabble.** A cool game to play is "Scrabble" using clippings from magazines. You cut out letters and then play "Scrabble" with the scraps.

5. **Word Pictures.** You can re-create a story with the words and pictures you cut from magazines. For example, you can cut out phrases, headlines, and key words, and then arrange them to create your own unique feature article or ad.

6. **Funny Faces.** Make a funny face using the nose from one photo, the eyes from another, and the hair from an animal—or whatever works for you. Every time we have done this with our kids it's a "cut up," and the results hang on our fridge. My favorite creation is a mish-mash face consisting of various celebrities, with the body of a super

model, riding a motorcycle.

7. **Dream On.** Create a collage of all the things you want to be, do, have when you grow up by ripping them out of magazines and catalogs. If that's too far out (in the future), try creating a dream board for all the things you want to do over summer vacation. (This isn't just for kids, by the way.)

WHAT YOU NEED

Scissors, glue, tape, and free publications.

Scavengers

55

A modern version of a scavenger hunt using a digital camera.

What child doesn't like an adventure? Here's a way to combine a kid's curiosity with their sense of adventure—and keep them busy for as long as needed. A scavenger hunt using a digital camera (or camera phone) can be used as a teaching tool depending on what you send the kids out to find. The game can also be played using a computer and Google.

HOW TO PLAY

1. Make a list of the things you want photographed (in order, if you want), and then set

some ground rules, which can include boundaries (don't cross the street, for instance) or a time limit, or just finish the list (if the football game is in the fourth quarter).

2. Make sure the players know how to use the camera or camera phone. (I know, the kids could probably show you the workings of the camera.)

3. Things on the list can be around the house, in the backyard, around the neighborhood, in the restaurant, outside the restaurant. The list can be people, places, things, whatever you want (or the kids want).

4. Play against the clock if you're on a limited schedule. Send players out to see who can gather the most items that start with a particular letter of the alphabet in under a minute. Or all things of a particular color in a set time frame.

WHAT YOU NEED

A camera phone or a digital camera, a time-keeping device, a computer or laptop.

BONUS

The game can also be played using a computer and a search engine like Google or an information source like Wikipedia. Make a list of questions such as who was the fourth U.S. President? What color were the snake's eyes in the *Jungle Book* movie? What team did Fletch play for in his NBA dream?

Science!

Here is your chance to conduct your own weird science experiments.

Learn a little about why things happen, scientifically that is. You may find you end up learning as much as your pupils. You may even learn what not to teach your kids about next time they ask!

HOW TO PLAY

1. **Sink or Float.** Using a large, clear bowl of water (or a glass), ask kids whether they think an item will sink or float. It sounds silly, but it's perfect for young children. You can take it a step further by asking them *why* a thing would sink or float.

2. **Plop, Plop, Fizz, Fizz.** You can start by finding a few pills in your purse. (We are not judging.) The best brand is Alka-Seltzer. Line up an aspirin, vitamin, and an Alka-Seltzer tablet and ask the kids what will happen when each is dropped in water. (They will love the bubbling action of Alka-Seltzer.) To show cause and effect (and learn a little about carbonation), shake a soda or sparkling water and allow them to open it.

3. **Operation.** Go fishing in a bowl full of odds and ends with tweezers or tongs (or chopsticks) and see what you can pull out without dropping it or hitting the sides. The person with the biggest pile at the end wins.

4. **Field Trip.** If you ask, you can usually take a behind-the-scenes tour of a restaurant or any other place where you find yourself with extra time. Especially with kids, people are usually willing to teach them about a business or how things are made or flown.

WHAT YOU NEED

Bowl with water.

Shooting Gallery

Using rubber bands and paper targets, kids can fire at will.

Rubber bands don't do damage, people do. Yes, you can poke an eye out when a rubber band is aimed incorrectly. That's why we propose the following semi-safe activity to help kids improve their aim and play a game at the same time. It's a shooting gallery for rubber bands. You can't get much safer than that right?

HOW TO PLAY

Rule number one is this: Never shoot a rubber band at another person. Ever (unless they really deserve it). Rule number two is the same as number one. Optional rule three is wear sunglasses if you can (plus you can look like *Men in Black*). Shooting a rubber band at a target, that's okay. So here's how to play. This game is played a lot like darts—but rubber bands are a lot less accurate—so your goal can be just to hit a target. As you get better, base it on points. You can make silhouettes of animals (this game is already politically incorrect, so we thought we'd just go ahead and go all the way) or of a person (see what we mean?). If you tape these targets up so they hang loosely, the rubber band usually makes a hole when it hits.

WHAT YOU NEED

Rubber bands, paper, tape, sunglasses, and a good aim.

Shopping Spree

58

A game to get others to correctly guess the costs of goods.

"Money doesn't grow on trees" was a common phrase we heard as kids. But isn't money made with paper, and doesn't paper come from trees? Anyway, it's true kids don't really know what things cost—until now.

HOW TO PLAY

1. **The Price Is Right.** Take the kids to the grocery store and find an item they know. Cover up the price and see how close they get to guessing the actual price. You'll all be amazed at how expensive toilet paper is.

2. **The Shopping Spree.** Give kids a calculator and an exact amount ($10.00) to spend at the store on whatever they want, as long as the total comes to within a few cents of the goal. They can't go over the $10. If they get it right, they can keep what they bought. If not, they will learn a valuable lesson about returns.

3. **Bargain Hunters.** Tell kids they have $20 to spend but must make it last because they have a three-item minimum—they must find at least three things for that price. This teaches them to look for good deals and markdowns.

4. **Shop Till You Drop.** While you shop for the items you need at the store, give kids a shopping list of their own (or drawings of items instead of an actual list). They will shop alongside you, carefully picking up the things they are supposed to get. Or, give them the list and a time to complete it while you wait at the magazine rack or coffee cart. Be careful assigning who gets eggs, spaghetti sauce, and milk on their list.

5. **Secret Shopper.** Teach kids about the joy of (gift) giving. Give each child a small amount of money and tell them to pick out a surprise gift for their father, mother,

brother, relative, or friend. The goal is to get the right gift (or a gag gift) based on the likes and dislikes of the recipient.

6. **Alphabet Soup Shopping.** Turn your grocery list into a learning tool by having your kids help you gather everything on the list—in alphabetical order. (Yes, it will take ten times as long to get what you need, but think of the fun you can have running around the store. Yeah, we know. That's why we made this suggestion the last one.)

WHAT YOU NEED

A calculator. A grocery store. And three hours for that last option.

Sock Me

Games and activities using your socks.

59

You may think socks are stinky things to stay away from—and generally speaking, they are (speak for yourself, Lee). But we have come up with a couple of clever ways to take something so simple (and smelly) and turn them into games and activities.

HOW TO PLAY

1. **Sock Hop.** The sock hop game is really simple. The first step is you have to take your shoes off—and have socks. Next, everyone is confined to a small area (preferably on grass, carpet, or sand—somewhere soft). Everyone starts with two socks. The object is to get the other players' socks off them. As long as you have two socks, you can

run. However, if you have a sock removed by another player, you can only hop on the foot with a sock. If you lose that last sock, you're out. Another version of this (which is better for small kids) is to have everyone seated with the (socked) feet meeting in the middle. Then, it's "game on" as you try to grab and remove each other's socks. The person with at least one sock left at the end wins. (It's even more fun when you play as teams.)

2. **I'm Your Puppet.** Using your sock as a hand puppet, you put on a play starring the members of your family. You imitate a sibling or parent, allowing your sock puppet to do the dirty work. Even draw on the socks with pens (if they're your parents' socks). Of course, you can put on a play with sock puppets, too.

WHAT YOU NEED

Socks. Soap and water for after you play—Peeeee Yoooooo.

Table Tennis Games

60

All you need to play these games is a hard surface and small ball.

These indoor sports are miniature versions of the real thing. You can actually play football, tennis, volleyball, and hockey with things found in your pocket or purse. Here are several examples.

HOW TO PLAY

1. **Table Tennis.** Here's a great way to play table tennis almost anywhere. All you need is a table, couple of plates (your paddles), a small ball (any ball will do), and piece of string tied to a salt or pepper shaker (your net), and you are playing ping pong.

2. **Hockey.** Any coin can serve as your puck. (Get several coins because you can keep the money you get in the "net.") Pencils or pens can serve as your hockey sticks (or use your fingers). The net can be anything from a hat to taped off area. Soccer can be played the same way with a small ball instead of a puck.

3. **Bocce Ball.** Player 1 slides out the target coin. Then the players take turns sliding their coins to the target one by one in turn. Closest coin to the target coin gets a point. He gets a second point if he has the second closest coin too. Play until someone reaches 11 points. Slide target from one side of the table to the other side, and add obstacles if you want.

4. **Pool.** A pencil with a nice new eraser can be the perfect pool cue. Now you'll need pool balls. Round vegetables work pretty well—but actual small balls are better. The pocket you will be trying to sink your shot into can be anything from a cup to a basket. You can also play to see who can get their ball closest to the "pin" (an object in the middle of the table).

5. **Football.** This is really a challenge for your field-goal kicking unit. The first step is to make your football by folding a piece of paper to form a small triangle (the "ball"). Next, you will need goal posts. These are easily created by having your opponent put their thumbs together and stick their index fingers straight up. You must then "kick" your ball by flicking it off the table with your finger. (You can be your own holder using one hand and flicking with the other, or have someone else hold it in place. See Hoop Dreams.)

WHAT YOU NEED

Pencils, paper, balls, string, coins.

Tag, You're It

61

Advertising is everywhere, and this is your chance to sell something.

Sometimes you feel like a nut, sometimes you don't. Just do it. Melts in your mouth, not in your hands. When put together, these sentences mean absolutely nothing. But individually, they are some of the most enduring product slogans of all time. We will use advertising (and popular television shows) to create some really cool games.

HOW TO PLAY

1. **Got Milk?** This is a simple game of trying to guess which slogan/tagline goes with which product or service. (You'll be surprised at just how many taglines you can re-

member and which company they go with.)

2. **Just Do It.** Create your own slogan for a product. Form a small team (your advertising agency) and see what kind of slogan you can come up with for existing products, or make some up. Choose the best one. Or, create your own commercial and act it out.

3. **Hey, Boo Boo.** Ever wonder why "The Professor" on *Gilligan's Island* could make a phone out of coconuts but couldn't fix the hole in the boat? Or, how come you can't remember what you had for dinner last night but can sing the entire Oscar Mayer baloney song? For this activity, see who can sing the most theme songs from popular television shows or commercials.

4. **Read All About It.** Write new (humorous) headlines or captions for photos, stories, or ads that appear in newspapers and magazines.

WHAT YOU NEED

Magazines, newspapers, catalogs, or access to a television.

Talent Show

62

If kids can sing and dance, do a cartwheel, handstand, or special cheer—it's a talent.

Not everyone is a "ham," but we all like watching one. So if someone in your family (or group) likes showing off, this will be a lot of fun. This activity can be done a lot of different ways depending on the preferences and "talents" of those participating. This can be a dance off, talent show, actor showcase, musical performance, air-guitar contest—or a combination of all the above. You will be surprised at how willing people are to show off their special "talent" when given a chance. Not only is this good for their self-esteem, it's entertaining for everyone else.

HOW TO PLAY

1. **American Idol.** If you want to do an *American Idol* type of show, give each person a chance to sing (or lip sync) to their favorite song. Some can do it a cappella (without instrumental accompaniment), others will want the music turned way up (karaoke like). When it comes to singing, there is safety in numbers. So, you can have a contest to see who is the best vocal group, or let the solo artists shine on their own. They can make up their own songs, or sing something from the radio—whichever is best. (You can also hold a songwriting contest.)

2. **Dance Off.** If you want to create a *Dancing with the Stars* contest, you can pair people off and see who does the best dance. (Of course, this is best done when music is playing, but it actually isn't entirely necessary.) Or, you can have a dance off in which individual participants do a dance by themselves. These will range from super to silly, but it's always a good time.

3. **Cheer Camp.** Cheerleading is serious stuff, but for this portion of the talent show,

anything goes. Funny works really well, but you can also "wow" the judges with your gymnastic moves. Or spirit fingers always work well too.

4. **Guitar Hero.** If nobody wants to sing and dance (or cheer), there is always the option to do an air-guitar rendition of a song. It's just as fun to add the air bass and air drums too. One of our favorites is the air tambourine. Let people pick their own special air instrument to make an entire air band.

5. **Night at the Improv.** Everyone's a comedian (or comedienne). Here's a chance to tell your best jokes (or make up some funny one-liners about those in the room) and try to get a laugh out of the audience. Or, this could be an open audition for aspiring actors. Start with a premise (you just won the Lottery!) and let the "actors" take it from there. Or, make it a combination of *What's My Line* and *Charades*, by handing out a slip of paper with a simple sentence on it and they have to act it out (you are a construction worker) and the audience tries to guess what it is. Start jack hammering away.

6. **America's Top Model.** Kids grab some of the adults' clothes (or switch with each

other), and then model them by prancing past the table as they make their way down the runway.

7. **X-Games.** Extreme sports like skateboarding are always entertaining to watch. Doctors love them too.

8. **Spelling Bee.** Maybe your kids are bookworms. So hold a spelling-bee contest.

WHAT YOU NEED

Music and a lot of chutzpah.

Toy Story

Show and tell (or sell) with toys.

In the movie *Toy Story*, the toys have minds of their own. What if your toys could talk, what would they say? Let's find out. Have you ever noticed how kids' cereal is positioned at the grocery store? (It's down low—eye level for children.) This time, instead of selling to kids, we're going to let the kids sell to us—or tell us a story with toys.

HOW TO PLAY

1. If toys could talk, what would they say? Let the kids create a whole story using their toys as props. Or create scenes and explain to you the history of a specific toy. Why they like it. What it does. Why I might like it. Who are the toy's friends. Just ask a lot

of questions to make the kids think up answers to get their brains going—try to keep them open ended—instead of true or false.

2. Have the kids sell something—like their toys—to the rest of the group. Be prepared to bargain for your favorite toys—or just the loud ones that you want to buy and hide where they can't be found again.

WHAT YOU NEED

Toys. Not cereal. A good hiding place.

Truth Or Dare

64

The wholesome version. In the right hands, these games can be good, clean fun.

Truth or Dare really is just a way to figure out who is the most daring or who has the most to hide. The "dare" part can be based on *Fear Factor* and *Survivor* (those who choose "dare" over "truth" must eat something gross—like spinach) or have to stand on one leg for a long time. Adults—you will definitely need to chaperone this one as you don't want the dares to become too disgusting or risky.

HOW TO PLAY

1. **Truth or Dare.** One person starts by asking another person a tough question while

at the same time coming up with a daring challenge. It's the player's choice which they want to do—answer the question or do the dare. Both the questions and the dares can be as easy or as hard as you wish.

2. **Spin the Bottle.** With everyone seated in a circle on the floor and a plastic bottle in the middle, the game begins. Players take turns spinning the bottle. When the bottle stops and points at a person, that person has to do what the person who spun it says to do. Again, remember what goes around, comes around.

3. **Post Office.** This game begins by having all the players think up a bunch of wild things to do. Then each activity is written on a small slip of paper and put in the "mailbox" (a hat or box). Players then take turns picking and must do what was on the piece of paper.

WHAT YOU NEED

Paper, pen, bottle, hat. Rules that limit dares and an adult to referee.

Twins

65

This is a cool way to find out how much you have in common with those around you.

We usually have more in common with others than we realize. These are games that celebrate our similarities rather than dwell on our differences. Then, there is the classic game where you must do exactly what "Simon" says.

HOW TO PLAY

1. If you're waiting in a long line with strangers, you can turn to someone and play this game to pass the time. Simply start by figuring out what you both like and dislike (food, music, movies, clothes, sports, hobbies, games). Then, see how much you look

alike (eyes, hair, skin color), and so on. Find all the things you have in common with the person sitting/standing next to you.

2. If you're part of a large group of people you know, break off into pairs and see which two people can find the most things in common in under two minutes. (Keep track.) If you want to make the game harder, you can limit the areas you focus on. For example, you can say, only find the things you have in common that have nothing to do with our family.

3. The game "Simon Says" has been around for years. What makes it a perennial favorite is how easy it is to play, but how hard it is to win. The game is simple, the leader (Simon) gives instructions to the other players like, "Simon says to touch your toes," or "Simon says to pick your nose." Everyone must follow orders. But, if the leader doesn't include a "Simon says" before giving an order, that means players aren't supposed to do it. If they do it anyway, they are out. So you have to listen carefully.

4. Simon with a twist—this is the same type of game only it's done with hand signals

or physical activities. All players must do exactly what Simon does. Like hop on one foot, or walk backwards, or wave their hands in the air. It's more of a follow-along type of game and the more silly things to mirror, the more the kids like to follow along.

WHAT YOU NEED

Yourself and your hand twin.

What's In Your Wallet?

A guessing game using items in your wallet, pocket, purse, or backpack.

Have you been meaning to clean out the contents of your purse? Here's your chance to do so. There are several ways to play, but the real winner will be the person whose wallet gets thinned down from a "George Costanza" to something more manageable.

HOW TO PLAY

Here are five different ways to play:

1. Three different people pick a few items to reveal from their pocket, purse, or wallet to put on the table (things not labeled with a person's name), and the rest of the group has to guess which items belong to which people.

2. Pull out all the items in your purse (or 10-12), and then put them back in and try to have the kids remember all the items they saw.

3. You can play the what-the-heck-is-this-doing-in-here game. The person who can pull out the weirdest, most outdated, or useless item from their wallet, purse, or backpack wins.

4. Cash is king, and the person who has the most, wins. First, everyone at the table tries to guess who they think has the most money in their wallet (coins count, too). The advanced version is to try and guess how much. See who was right. Play the game with adults—whoever has the most money buys the next round.

5. A person looks at an item in their purse and gives clues about it while others guess what it might be.

WHAT YOU NEED

Confidence in spilling your guts out to everyone because everyone now knows you are what's in your purse. This is going to be fun!

Worst-Case Scenario

67

What would you do if you were in the middle of an emergency—let's find out.

Come up with several scenarios and ask kids what they would do. They can be good or bad-case scenarios. Imagine a dream world where anything is possible and everyone had the best intentions, now think up some great inventions.

HOW TO PLAY

1. **What if You . . .** The leader of this exercise should be a person who believes the

glass is not only half empty, but too small as well. Here's why—one person will come up with some seriously scary scenarios and ask participants what they would do. The person who answers the best, wins.

2. **What if We . . .** Tell the players to imagine that anything is possible. Now, ask them to invent something that would make the world a better place—or their lives easier.

3. **What if It's . . .** This activity is all about teaching kids to troubleshoot and learn how things work—with adult supervision. Unplug an appliance or remove a light bulb and see if kids can find out why it won't work. Or draw a picture of something and purposely draw one part wrong to see who can point it out.

4. **What the . . .** Close your eyes and guess the smell, sound, or thing touching you.

WHAT YOU NEED

A pessimist. And a few optimists to try and turn him/her around.

Word Games

We will prove the power of the pen—and how it can make time fly by.

It was said that the pen is mightier than the sword—if it were shot from a cannon. The truth is, word games like crossword puzzles and "Scrabble" have been entertaining people since Gutenberg invented the printing press. (That's a stretch, which is another game you can play with a pen and paper.) Here are some word games, but there are many more you can find (or invent) on your own, too.

HOW TO PLAY

1. **Words within a Word.** Write down a sentence and set a time limit to find out how

many other words you can find within the sentence. You can also use several random letters to find out how many words can be made using them. The person who finds the most words is the winner. Or you can give points for words of different lengths—3 points for three-letter words and 5 points for five-letter words. The player with the most points wins, and then they get to write down a new sentence. Or have an adult be the designated sentence writer. Create your own word-search game using something only the people in the room would get—family names, family vacations, middle names. Or, scramble up the sentence or letters and try to put them back into the correct order. Have themes based on the restaurant you're in, or the meal you'll soon be eating. Here is yet another way to have fun with words. Find words with more than one meaning (rack, stack, whack) or (a horn on a car, a horn on an animal, a horn in a band). See who can come up with the most words with more than one meaning.

2. **Picture Words.** Take ordinary items (or drawings of them) and turn them into sentences or statements. For example, "an eye for an eye" is a statement that could be

created with two eyes, the number four, and half an ant (for the "an" part). By creating sentences with pictures of animals or objects, you can create a secret code of communication. Think of a sentence you want to draw, and draw a picture for each word. Then pass it around to see who can solve it in the fastest time possible. Another way to play is to draw pictures of people, places, or things and have others guess who it is—like Pictionary. Or cut out pictures from magazines to create sentences—like a ransom note, but ask for cookies instead of a billion dollars.

WHAT YOU NEED

Paper and pencil/pen/crayons. A fine mastery of the English language (i.e., passing of the second grade).

Write On

69

Become a journalist or author and get the scoop and tell the story.

Interview a person in your family (or a stranger) and write an article about them—and then read it aloud or e-mail it to everyone later. Not only does the interviewer learn a lot, but the interviewee will love it too—they get to share their life story with a loved one. There is also a chance to collaborate with your friends and family to write a short story. Read on.

HOW TO PLAY

1. **The Journalist.** Many journalists use nothing more than a notepad and a pen to

conduct their interviews. That's all that's necessary here—although you can go high-tech, too, and use a digital recorder or a camera. The first step is to assign a "reporter" (someone in the group) to do an in-depth interview of a person about their past. The interviewer pretends to be a journalist and asks the tough questions ("If you were a tree, what kind of tree would you be?" or "What was your favorite thing to do when you were younger?"). While one person is pretending to be a reporter, the one being interviewed can pretend to be a movie star, a superhero, or a famous athlete. You can then try to guess who the person being interviewed is, and have the other people at the table help, too, based on their answers to your questions. You could create a "who dunnit?" scenario and try to get clues out of the interviewee to solve the crime. The basic way to play is to write a short biography about them for a newspaper or magazine article, and read it out loud when you are done.

2. **The Writer.** They say everyone has a story to tell and at least one book in them. Well, we're about to find out if that's true. We are going to start a story and let each

person in the room add a sentence or two to what was written previously. The object is to keep the story the same, even though the "manuscript" is moving around the room. The story starts with one sentence: "It was a dark and stormy night . . ." or "Once upon a time . . ." and then the paper is passed to the next person to add the next sentence. The story makes its way around and around the room until it's done. Then someone reads the entire tale aloud.

WHAT YOU NEED

Pen, paper, and your imagination—it's that easy.

Zip It

70

This is a scavenger hunt using a small baggie to collect your treasures.

Create a list of items to find—the difficulty can be varied depending on the age of those searching. This game can occupy the little ones for more than a few minutes while they spend time trying to fill their baggies; give prizes for lists finished. It's amazing what kids will do for a small bag of M&Ms.

HOW TO PLAY

Find a theme for the items on the list—things around the house, flowers and leafs, foods, etc. The difficulty can range depending on the patience of those searching or the amount of time you are trying to fill. You can set a time limit and the one with the most objects wins, or the first one back with all the items in the bag wins. You can also set the order in which items may be found and have one group time the next.

WHAT YOU NEED

Paper and pens to create lists, and plastic bags to house all the found treasures.

BONUS

Play in the house and collect only food items. Then at the end, you get to eat your treasure. Or, you can collect items that can be reused for another activity in this book (i.e., search for items to stack on your wrist for the Backhanded Compliment). An added bonus for football watchers—if you are looking for a snack while watching the game at home on the couch, add a pizza coupon, phone, and wallet to the search list, and when the searchers return . . . Voilá, instant delivery!

SMART FUN

We have literally put every single activity in this book to the test and the benefits listed here are the real deal. By playing the games in this book, we (and our family and friends) found ourselves laughing, learning, and wondering where the time went. We also discovered firsthand this isn't just about fun and games and beating boredom. You and your kids will also increase your: artistry, creativity, financial intelligence, fine-motor skills, focus, friendship, genealogy, geography, goals, history, math, medical terms, memory, patience, physiology, political saavy, problem solving, resourcefulness, scientific knowledge, self-confidence, sportsmanship, talents, teamwork, thriftiness, and timing.

WHEN-U-GO
SAFE FUN

No kids were harmed (much) in the making of this book, in part because we were very careful (and lucky). It's all fun and games until someone gets hurt. That's why we want to warn everyone reading and using this book to be cautious when horsing around. Anticipate the worst-case scenario before it happens, and take steps to avoid it. Be as carefree as you can while playing, but also as careful as you can when preparing to play—and when someone yells duck, do it (see Musical Menus). That's our way of saying . . . have fun, but don't hurt your parents in the process.

LEE SILBER

Lee Silber is the author of 14 other books and the 2002 winner of the Theodor S. Geisel Award for outstanding writing. Several years ago, Lee started keeping a loose-leaf binder of all the creative ways he was able to entertain kids of all ages—using simple, ordinary items. In time, he realized he possessed a book that would quickly help other adults become the favorite parent, relative, or friend. This became especially important after October 21, 2004—which is the date Lee and his wife had their first of two children. As predicted by those closest to him, Lee is now very interested in writing books that benefit kids (and parents).

MIKE METZ

Mike Metz is a graduate of Cal Poly San Luis Obispo with a B.S. in Graphic Communications. Mike has always been known for his creativity. As a sales executive for a global shareholder communications firm, he is renowned in the industry for coming up with clever and creative ways to make his sales events both fun and functional. A competitive volleyball player, an avid surfer, and all-around sports enthusiast, Mike made sure the sports-related games included in this book would work for kids of all levels. Mike's wife of 14 years is a California Teacher-of-the-Year Award winner. They are the parents of two children. The Metz family have battle-tested the ideas in this book—under the most extreme conditions—and they all worked.

WRITE-E-O

FREE STUFF

While we both agree the activities in this book are fantastic just as they are written, (and that's not just because we wrote them), we suggest you take these ideas and make them your own. In fact, we encourage you to send us your ideas, experiences, and feedback for possible inclusion in the sequel. Also, contact us to get your free booklet filled with more fun from your pocket and purse. Finally, *Bored Games* is available as a fundraising tool and we (the authors) are available to speak at functions.

www.leesilber.com

leesilber@earthlink.net